"Revival is a word that is often misunde.......... it describes that life—and that Church—marked by an ever-present encounter with Jesus, which results in a passion to reflect His glory, experience His presence and obey His commission. Revival is a lifestyle, not an event. Rare are the writers who speak to the issue of sustaining such a state. Yet it is the crux of where we are as a Church today. Alistair Petrie has done what few have—given us a comprehensive strategy grounded in timeless principles designed to help us walk in a perpetual state of genuine revival.

Like a master weaver, he threads together key strands of truth that, when viewed as a whole, present us with a tapestry of dynamic spiritual life and successful mission. Passionate prayer, humble leadership, the pursuit of unity, even the vital (and often neglected) concept of dealing with root sins that for generations have defiled the very land on which we live—all are stitched together in brilliant interplay.

This book is a manual for living in sustained encounter with God's presence, to which we will need to refer again and again."

Steve Fry, president, Messenger Fellowship
author, *Rekindled Flame*

"Alistair Petrie has provided us with a foundational and cutting-edge book on how to steward God's presence in revival. Transformed! clearly reveals the privilege and responsibility God places on His people to birth and sustain revival in the land. It will challenge and encourage you to assume your place in the destiny of your city and nation."

Jean Steffenson, president
Native American Resource Network

"*Transformed!* transmutes lessons learned from the agonies of moves of God truncated in past times into initiatives, in order to steward more wisely the precious oil of renewal when it flows. Petrie gleans for us the errors of revivals past and shares viable correctives for what we long for God to do in here-and-now cities and nations. One thing was clear to me in this read—that the Spirit of God is appointing and anointing leaders, prayer warriors, and men and women in the marketplace, putting in place an infrastructure of spiritual leadership that is geo-specific. Alistair shares with those bringing about new wineskins of God's presence vital instruction on how to preserve the fullness of the life of Jesus poured out in special seasons of visitation. May this book be in great demand and jump off the shelves in the days ahead."

Tom White, president
Frontline Ministries

"Alistair Petrie's new book is about revival, full of carefully researched wisdom and based on a wealth of priceless experience. Every church leader should read it—not just to learn about revival, but to understand the prevailing conditions that are necessary for a local fellowship to become and remain a "normal" Christian church, alive and fulfilling the purposes of God irrespective of time or circumstance."

Peter Horrobin, international director
Ellel Ministries International

"We often question why revivals come and go. This book is the result of vast research to answer that question. Alistair Petrie delves into historic and modern transcultural revivals, as well as the Scriptures, to present the reader with the answer. I highly recommend this book for all those who are not satisfied with times of revival, but desire to see the Lord penetrate society, transforming its very structure."

Dr. Ruth J. Ruibal, international conference speaker, author
pastor, Ekklesia Centro Cristiano Colombiano, Cali, Colombia

Transformed!

PEOPLES • CITIES • NATIONS

*10 Principles
for Sustaining
Genuine Revival*

ALISTAIR P. PETRIE

Chosen Books

A Division of Baker Book House Co
Grand Rapids, Michigan 49516

Published by Chosen Books
A division of Baker Book House Company
P.O. Box 6287, Grand Rapids, MI 49516-6287
www.bakerbooks.com

Printed in the United States of America

Library of Congress Cataloging-in-Publication Data
Petrie, Alistair P., 1950–
    Transformed! : 10 principles for sustaining genuine revival / Alistair P.
Petrie.
        p. cm.
    Includes bibliographical references and index.
    ISBN 0-8007-9337-4 (pbk.)
    1. Revivals. I. Title.
BV3790 .P486 2003
269′ .2—dc21   2002153295

To my dear wife, Marie—

Thanks for sharing the journey with me, honey!

And to the Lord Himself whose presence goes with us, and who gives us His rest—the One who calls, appoints, anoints and never disappoints!

Contents

Acknowledgments

I have been hidden away for the last several days in a beautiful part of Vancouver Island. I am surrounded by books, papers, tapes and a magnificent view of oceans, mountains and trees. What an extraordinary setting in which to write a book that deals with the glory of God. However, this would not be possible without the encouragement, patience and prayers of many people working with me on this project. In particular I would like to thank my dear wife, Marie, for her ongoing encouragement and belief that this project is a timely tool for the Church. Thank you, Marie—you have been incredible! I also want to thank my sons, Mike and Richard, and my wonderful daughter-in-law, Anna. They are amazing in their support and prayers for a dad who seems to be either going to or coming from the airport. Thanks, Richard, for looking after the grass during these days!

I also want to thank many of my friends and colleagues in ministry worldwide for their ongoing support, encouragement and inspiration. Peter and Doris Wagner, Mike and Cindy Jacobs, Steve and Nancy Fry, Ruth Ruibal, John Robb, David Demian, Peter Horrobin, Jean Steffensen and Chuck Pierce are but a few who come to mind. "As iron sharpens iron, so one man sharpens another" (Proverbs 27:17). I have valued the support and wisdom of the members of my Sentinel Canada Board and my Joshua Connection Board, along with the prayers of many intercessors who faithfully care for Marie and me as we travel to many different—and sometimes challenging—destinations. My thanks and blessings to you all.

Once again I am indebted to Helen Thornton who has so faithfully and diligently typed and re-typed manuscripts for me over a number of years, and also to her husband, Errol. Both have been an invaluable part of this project.

A special thanks again to my mother and father, and two "much older" brothers who taught me to appreciate the adventure of life. Those early train rides have given me cherished memories.

Love and blessings,
APP

Foreword

There is a consensus among Christian leaders with whom I associate that a season of great revival, most likely an outpouring of the Holy Spirit unprecedented in Christian history, is just around the corner. I believe it will happen in this generation. I am not sure that many people my age (I am in my eighth decade of life) will live to see it, but I am convinced that the majority of people alive today will.

I do not have an exact count, but I would guess that we have been hearing more reports of revival over the past ten years than we heard during the one hundred years preceding. Those with an ear to hear what the Spirit is saying to the churches are agreeing that these signs, scattered across the globe as they are, bear a divine message for our age. No one who reads the Scriptures could doubt that it is God's will to pour out widespread revival on His people. If it has not happened as yet, why not?

The answer to this must relate to timing. Our sovereign, omnipotent God has chosen to interact personally with the people He created in such a way that some of His actions are contingent on what His people actually decide to do. Deuteronomy 28, for example, contains a long list of blessings and a long list of curses. The point of the chapter: that God can go either way. He can and will release blessings, and He can and will release curses. The variable is whether His people obey His voice. It is important to understand that the choice is not God's; it is ours.

This relates directly to the great revival God desires to send to us. We, God's people, have some critical choices to make. It is true that God has sent many outstanding revivals in the past. Elmer Towns and Douglas Porter list some of them in The Ten Greatest Revivals Ever (Servant, 19xx). But it is also true that, throughout history, the period of true revival fire was, more often than not, relatively short-lived. I would think that God wants this next revival to be different. I would think He wants "[His] will done on earth as it is in heaven," as Jesus taught us to pray; not to be a flash in the pan but to transform the societies in which we live on a long-term basis.

What, then, is God waiting for? What are we to do in order to see God's revival blessings released? At least one of the things, very possibly the main one, that God is waiting for is to be sure that His people understand and are prepared to implement the principles, the attitudes, the structures and the behavior patterns necessary to sustain revival. That is what this book is all about.

I am thoroughly delighted that Alistair Petrie has written Transformed! The usual theme of a book on revival is "Lord, please come!" I have 65 books on revival in my personal library, and most of the content of these books—say, 99 percent of it—deals with initiating the revival, not sustaining it when it comes. Charles Finney's classic Lectures on Revivals of Religion, for example, is one of the few that even brings up the matter of sustaining revival, and only twelve pages out of a total of 455 (or two percent) are devoted to the subject.

The book you hold in your hand is the only one I am aware of that deals entirely with sustaining revival. It could well be that this will turn out to be the catalyst that releases the hand of God to pour out the great revival. But the choice is still ours. If we absorb what Alistair has shared with us, if we gain agreement throughout the Body of Christ that these principles are vital, and if we decide to pay the price and do whatever is necessary to lay the strong foundations for sustaining revival, we can realistically expect God's enormous outpouring to come sooner rather than later.

C. Peter Wagner
Colorado Springs, Colorado

Introduction

I love trains! As a young boy growing up in Scotland I always experienced a sense of adventure and anticipation whenever my parents, brothers and I set off on a train journey. My adrenaline system went on high alert. Stepping onto the train, I felt as if I was about to explore another world. After being seated in the compartment, it was time to investigate what lay behind and in front of me. Of course, the biggest excitement was getting close to the engine, especially when we went through a tunnel. The sounds of the whistle and huge locomotive wheels thundering upon the tracks and echoing against the walls and then the smell of the smoke were pure excitement for this young lad! Years later I experienced my first Canadian train ride. I was amazed at the length of the train and the different cars—the sleeping cars, the dining and lounge cars, the entertainment and day cars—all different and yet all part of the same train heading in the same direction. I was in my element.

I still love adventures, I still love going on journeys, and I still love trains. The journeys I now undertake are somewhat different, but the destination is always the same. Since *Releasing Heaven on Earth* was published, I have continued in the direction of that journey. I visit communities, cities and nations that are seeking their destiny in the Lord. In that vein, I am witnessing a growing sense of anticipation and expectation all over the world. Winds of revival are blowing, and a sense of nearing our destination is on the increase. Although the journey is not yet complete, this book expresses what has been on my heart for several years—my discovery of the principles I believe God is instilling into His Church today so that we can welcome His transforming power into our lives, the lives of our cities and even that of our nations. The result will be a release of His presence and His glory upon our lives.

This book is not about the subject and experience of revival *per se*. Many excellent books are available on that subject—I am presently surrounded by almost forty of them here in my office! While I will review some definitions and examples of revival as it has occurred in various times and places, I will be selective. Rather, this book is a response to questions I have asked—and personally been asked by others all over the world. Most expressly, I attempt to answer the question, *When revival comes, why does it leave?*

It has been an exciting journey, discovering the answers to that question, and in many ways as thrilling as my early journeys on those trains. Just as each component of the train was essential in order for everyone to arrive at his destination, I believe the principles in this book all are essential for us to apply with care, determination and volumes of prayer if we want to fall in love with the presence of God and bask in His glory. If this satisfies a hunger and passion that you have for the glory of God, then read on.

Authentic revival should lead to transformation, which is a continual process of people and society being changed into an ever-deepening relationship with God. However, history teaches us that revival rarely lasts long enough for authentic transformation to take place. On my journey, I have discovered ten reasons why this is the case and what needs to be done to steward revival so that it does indeed lead to authentic transformation.

Each principle I will address is rather like arriving at a station. Sometimes we will spend longer in one place than another. But all of these principles are interdependent. They all are required if we want to take an intimate look at the heart of God and the destiny He has planned for us.

Using history as a tutor and examining these ten principles of stewardship, we will learn how the presence of God can penetrate every part of life and society today, so that the glory of the Lord indeed finds a resting place in the midst of His people. We will look at the subject of persevering leadership and see how this is a critical component for both the release and the stewarding of revival. We will see that the presence of God is attracted to certain factors found in persevering leaders—holiness, humility and unity. We will learn what it means to pay the price of being a persevering leader—and still survive! Then we will examine the principle of prevailing prayer. Not only is it an essential ingredient for releasing God's transforming power in the land, but it requires a willingness to be discomforted and inconvenienced if we are going to listen to the Lord and pray in such a way that we are not distracted by worldly issues or challenges. Prevailing prayer requires a level of tenacity fueled by expectancy that is willing to undertake whatever spiritual wrestling matches may come on the journey toward community transformation.

History records that many revivals end when our intimacy with God is compromised. This occurs because we lose a sense of holiness and intimacy with the Lord, and we no longer live and work in the fear of the Lord. It is the fear of the Lord that helps us address the issues of sin that so readily short-circuit revivals. Sin is sometimes subtle and at other times horrifically blatant, but it needs to be addressed if the Church is to be the prophetic voice of

God in society today. In her role as the authoritative sign of the Kingdom of God in the world, the Church carries the responsibility of dealing with seeds of sin, roots of disease and any fruit of complaint and complacency that arises. We undertake this "spiritual agriculture" in order that no "little foxes" are given freedom in the vineyard.

As we continue this journey we will see that the Church is called to steward the territory that is entrusted to us— to guard, keep and occupy what rightfully belongs to the Lord. This involves restoring lost boundaries and misplaced foundations. Often, revival has ended or entered into a type of "spiritual receivership" because the foundations for a lasting revival simply were not there in the first place. It is our responsibility to protect the seeds of revival and to prepare for a harvest. As stewards of revival we will learn that those to whom much has been given, much will be required.

We will then look at the principle of unity. Using my analogy of the train, each car is linked to the other with couplings that ensure one car will not separate from another when being pushed or pulled by the engine. This also means that the heat and the air brake systems are transferred throughout the entire length of the train. Each car must be linked correctly to the next in order that no weakness or malfunction occurs that could affect the entire train. There is, therefore, an overall state of interdependency—or unity—existing throughout the entire train. Much has been written and taught on this subject of unity over the years, but we will take a unique perspective by viewing it in terms of revival and the release of God's presence and glory. Sometimes unity requires division—we will find out why.

We will also visit the A.O.K. principle. Every authentic revival has been accompanied and sometimes even preceded by Acts of Kindness. In Scripture we read of the compassion of Jesus that touched and transformed the lives of people. True revival should lead to deeper and ongoing care of the impoverished in society, which can turn a city and even a nation toward Christ.

We also will turn our attention to the subject of watchmen and the responsibility entrusted into their care (see Isaiah 62:6–7). We will see why the stewarding of revival requires the extension of watchmen. Are watchmen the same as gatekeepers? We will see why gatekeeping today requires a review of the subject of leadership and the role of the apostle. Finally, we will address how to establish revival in society so that it has a lasting influence. This requires fresh vision, new wineskins and the positioning of our young people to affect the generations of today and tomorrow. I have heard George Barna quoted as saying the average wineskin for the Church lasts three to five years before it requires renewing. God requires His Church to continue to develop new wineskins so that we are prepared for tomorrow's new wine. We need to share the biblical message in such a way that no one misses the destination: authentic transformation and the glory of God coming upon us.

Our journey begins. If we can take these principles of stewardship into consideration, then revival can become authentic transformation and will result in the release of God's glory in our midst. The Church in the twenty-first century is being positioned into a new level of authority and authenticity—to rise and walk in the midst of adversity and challenge. We are familiar with the following well-known passage:

> If my people, who are called by my name, will humble themselves and pray and seek my face and turn from their wicked ways, then will I hear from heaven and will forgive their sin and will heal their land.
>
> 2 Chronicles 7:14

But it is the next two verses that testify to the Lord's presence in our midst:

> Now my eyes will be open and my ears attentive to the prayers offered in this place. I have chosen and consecrated this temple so that my Name may be there forever. My eyes and my heart will always be there.
>
> 2 Chronicles 7:15–16

If this is on your heart today, then let's start the journey. The destination? As Zechariah 8 indicates, when the presence of the Lord dwells in our midst, the city will be called the City of Truth (verse 3), and many people and powerful nations will come and seek the Lord in that city (verse 22). May each one of us, our cities and our nations enter fully into this destiny He has purposed for us.

> For the earth will be filled with the knowledge of the glory of the LORD, as the waters cover the sea.
>
> Habakkuk 2:14

May it happen soon, Lord!

Rev. Dr. Alistair P. Petrie
British Columbia, Canada

1

...

The World Is Being Prepared

The business of the truth is not to be deserted even to the sacrifice of our lives, for we live not for this age of ours, nor for the princes, but for the Lord.

Zwingli

We are probably living in the most extraordinary time of recorded history. Dramatic changes are taking place all over the world on a scale that often defies human understanding. The world will never be the same again following the events of September 11, 2001—commonly known as 9/11. On that day, the "age of innocence" abruptly came to an end. Politics, the economy, issues dealing with personal and national security, and even the message of the Church at large all took on a new sense of urgency and interpretation. Suddenly, the status quo of life was interrupted!

Up until 1997, my family and I had spent many years pastoring churches in England, Scotland and Canada. These years were of immense importance to me, as I came to appreciate God's call on the local church fellowship to be the sign of the Kingdom of God in the local community. Since 1997 I have had the wonderful privilege of serving the Lord in many nations of the world through my relationships with various ministry organizations. Wherever I go, I hear the same message on the lips of Christians, whether they are serving God in a leadership capacity or on the mission field or as members of the Body of Christ appropriating their Christian witness in their day-to-day work. The question is very simple: "Revival—can it happen here?" This is a question I myself also asked many times during my years in residential pastoring.

During a recent visit to Norway, I worked with a number of Norwegian church leaders. They believe that God is positioning their nation for a national revival. While there, I was given a Christian newsletter published by the Shetland Prayer Link, a group located on the Shetland Islands off the northern tip of the Scottish mainland toward the Norwegian Sea. Even in that remote part of the world the central theme of this newsletter was once again "Revival—can it happen here?" In fact, the question has begun to change into more of a statement of expectancy. Whether I am in Singapore, Malaysia, South Africa, Australia, New Zealand, Norway, the United States, Canada or the United Kingdom, I recognize that leadership has been positioned for a dramatic move of the presence of God upon the face of this earth. It is as if God has instilled into the hearts and minds of people all over the world that He is about to move on a level for which many of us have hoped but that few people in this generation have ever really experienced. We are indeed living in amazing and extraordinary days!

Is Revival Synonymous with Renewal?

Just what is revival anyway? Many people feel that revival is synonymous with renewal. This is not the case at all. It is true that certain dynamics of renewal are similar to revival. In my library I have a copy of the April or May 1986 *Renewal* magazine, published by Anglican Renewal Ministries in England. The featured article for that particular edition deals with the subject of what renewal is—and what it is not. The article states that renewal is about being filled with the Holy Spirit, along with a switch from dependence on natural talent to the seeking of God's power. It is a discovery of the gifts of grace that God has for His people. It is enrichment by the fruit of the Spirit and empowerment by the gifts of the Spirit.

The article also states that renewal is a fundamental work of the Holy Spirit to glorify Jesus, often involving a discovery of praise, adoration, thanksgiving, worship and joy that reveals Jesus' working in us and through us with fresh passion and urgency. When a church experiences such renewal, the people experience a heightened desire to share the word and work of Christ with others. In other words, there is a genuine awakening of the people of God toward the needs and concerns of a broken and divided body. In the same magazine, the well-known British Bible teacher David Pawson is quoted as saying, "Renewal is walking in the Spirit, in the light, in love and in a way that is worthy of our calling."[1]

Frank Damazio, meanwhile, defines *renewal* as "the receiving of new Holy Spirit activity into a hungry soul and allowing the Holy Spirit to bring inner refreshing and remodeling of the soul as it seeks after God. Renewal is the receiving of a new life and new fire into the soul of a person, a church or a city."[2] Damazio sees *revival* as only part of what he refers to as eight stages to "revival rivers":

renewal, receiving, refining, recovering, reforming, resisting, reaching, reaping, then revival. Each stage is part of an ongoing cycle of change mixed with joys, tribulations, challenges, conflicts and breakthroughs. Each needs adopting in order to cross into the revival rivers.[3]

Damazio says, "Revival . . . is a word to describe the ongoing state of a healthy church, a church with a wide river, a river that takes in from other rivers but maintains its own river distinctives. When biblical distinctives are maintained, a church may live with a powerful, fresh, flowing river of God.[4]

Definitions of Authentic Revival

Damazio's definition is only a partial explanation and description of authentic revival. Dr. Martyn Lloyd-Jones described revival in the following way:

It is an experience in the life of the Church when the Holy Spirit does an unusual work. He does that work primarily amongst the members of the Church; it is *a reviving of the believers* [emphasis mine]. You cannot revive something that has never had life, so revival, by definition, is first of all an enlivening and quickening and awakening of lethargic, sleeping, almost moribund Church members. Suddenly, the power of the Spirit comes upon them, and they are brought into a new and more profound awareness of the truths they had previously held intellectually, and perhaps at a deeper level too. They are humbled, they are convicted of sin . . . and then they come to see the great salvation of God in all its glory and to feel its power. Then, as a result of their quickening, they begin to pray. New power comes into the preaching of the ministers and the result of this is that large numbers who were previously outside the church are converted and brought in.[5]

In his book *In Pursuit of His Glory*, Gerald Fry says, "Revival is not an event. It is a process God uses to change our lives, to draw us into a deeper, more confident relationship with Him so that we might reflect His glory." He then quotes his friend Joy Dawson, who defined revival in this way: "Revival is the full manifestation of the life of Christ in every believer. Revival is God stirring, shaking and changing His Church from apathy to passion for Christ, from indifference to humility, from idolatry to holiness."[6]

In His book *Finney on Revival,* V. Raymond Edman quotes Charles Finney as saying:

> A revival consists of Christians being renewed in their first love, resulting in the awakening and conversion of sinners to God. In the popular sense, a revival of religion in a community is the awakening, quickening and reclaiming of the backslidden church and the general awakening of all classes, ensuring a tension to the claims of God. . . . Revival is the coming of the inexpressibly sweet and tender Spirit of God into the midst of His people with convicting and transforming power. The outpouring of God's Spirit is the divine aspect of revival, while the preparation of the heart is our part.[7]

Although Colin Dye, senior minister of Kensington Temple in London, implies that the word *revival* is not found anywhere in the Bible, he does admit that Scripture records several examples and principles of revival.[8] In fact, the Old and the New Testaments contain more than fifty references to the term *revival* and its various synonyms, giving insight to God's perspective on this expression of His relationship with His people. For example, Psalm 85:6–7 reads: "Will you not *revive* us again, that your people may rejoice in you? Show us your unfailing love, O LORD, and grant us your salvation" (emphasis mine). This verse implies a longing to return to an earlier place of intimacy and passion in a people's relationship with the living God.

Over the last several centuries, many revivals have exemplified a consistent yearning on the part of the people of God to return to a Pentecost experience like that recorded in Acts 2. Charles Finney once said, "The antecedents, accompaniments and results of revivals are always substantially the same as in the case of Pentecost."[9] Whether on an individual or corporate basis, revival indicates a visitation from God that returns the people to an experience of God's presence, holiness and intimacy that characterized their relationship with Him at an earlier time. Certainly, during such periods as the Welsh Revival of 1904 and the Ulster Revival of 1859, many non-believers came to Christ. These conversion outcomes are why such visitations from God are sometimes referred to as "awakenings." They are a product of genuine revival; when the local church is revived, the harvest begins within the surrounding community of non-believers. There is no doubt about it: When revival takes place, the result is a season of powerful visitation from God affecting initially the believers in the local church, subsequently the ingathered church in a collective area, and ultimately the entire community. Jesus Himself did promise, "When I am lifted up from the earth, [I] will draw all men to myself" (John 12:32).

The heart-cry of the people of God is found in Exodus 33:

"If your Presence does not go with us, do not send us up from here. How will anyone know that you are pleased with me and with your people unless you go with us? What else will distinguish me and your people from all the other people on the face of the earth?" . . . Then Moses said, "Now show me your glory."

Exodus 33:15–16, 18

From the early days of the Old Testament, God's desire has been to establish His presence *in the midst* of His people so that His people can declare His honor and glory to all the nations of the world. Even God Himself says, "I will cause all my goodness to pass in front of you, and I will proclaim my name, the Lord, in your presence" (Exodus 33:19).

Similar to Charles Finney's statement is a statement by Martyn Lloyd-Jones: "Every revival is a repetition of Pentecost, and it is the greatest need of the Christian Church at this present hour."[10] Revival, therefore, is never an event in itself, but rather, "It is the process God uses to change our lives, to draw us into a deeper, more confident relationship with Him so that we might reflect His glory."[11] It is the glory of God and the goodness of God reflected within the lives of His people. Paul the apostle says we are mirrors of God's glory: "Now the Lord is the Spirit, and where the Spirit of the Lord is, there is freedom. And we, *who with unveiled faces all reflect the Lord's glory,* are being transformed into his likeness with ever-increasing glory, which comes from the Lord, who is the Spirit" (2 Corinthians 3:17–18, emphasis mine). Revival, simply explained, brings the people with unveiled faces before the almighty God so that we might *reflect* His glory.

But authentic revival goes even further. Since "God has chosen to bless His Church with the fullness of the Holy Spirit on the condition of its moving toward certain vital norms of health and witness,"[12] revival becomes the complete spiritual revitalization within the Church and all its various programs. Therefore, God's people not only *return* to a place of intimacy with the Lord, but they also move *toward* a degree of health and normality that God requires of His Church in order for His purpose and message to be declared unto all the nations of the earth. The Church in revival is able to carry out this mandate in a fashion that brings the Lord complete honor and glory.

The Reverend Duncan Campbell on Revival

Off the far northwest coast of the Scottish mainland are the Outer Hebrides Islands. Two of these islands, Lewis and Harris, have experienced various spiritual awakenings over the years, especially from 1940–1953. In 1949 the Reverend Duncan Campbell responded to a call from God and the local church in Barvas, a small community on the Isle of Lewis, to spend several days in that area. In the community of Barvas, at that time, a number of people had been waiting on the Lord and sensed He was about to move in great power throughout their island. This is exactly what took place following the arrival of Duncan Campbell, who would be the first to say that he did not bring revival to the Hebrides. God already had been at work on the island prior to his arrival, but he became a vital catalyst for this move of God for the next three years. Duncan Campbell gave his definition of revival:

> First, let me tell you what I mean by revival. An evangelistic campaign or special meeting is not revival. In a successful evangelistic campaign or crusade, there will be hundreds or even thousands of people making decisions for Jesus Christ, but the community remains untouched, and the churches continue much the same as before the outreach. In revival, God moves in the district. Suddenly, the community becomes God-conscious. The Spirit of God grips men and women in such a way that even work is given up as people give themselves to waiting upon God. . . . This presence of God is the supreme characteristic of the God-sent revival. . . . The power of God, the Spirit of God, was moving in operation, and the fear of God gripped the souls of men—this is God-sent revival as distinct from special efforts in the field of evangelism.[13]

All of the above-mentioned working definitions of revival have come from the lives and ministries of people who have been involved in actual revival. Revival has to do with the people of God themselves. But at the same time thousands of souls can be saved through revival when the power of God's presence comes upon spiritually dry ground. As Duncan Campbell also said, "If you want revival, get right with God. . . . It is about time we got into the grips of reality. Are we thirsty?"[14] When we have revival, the thirsty are satisfied. However, we now have to ask another question: Is revival the same as transformation?

Is Revival Synonymous with Transformation?

George Otis is president of the Sentinel Group, a Christian research ministry that investigates the spiritual dynamics at work in cities and territories. The ministry identifies corporate spiritual strongholds and seeks appropriate ways to remove them. The Sentinel Group then documents the efforts of local Christians in preparing their community for a visitation of the Holy Spirit.

Otis likens the transforming power of God to molten lava that literally affects everything in its path as it descends upon a community. When God's presence enters into the community through the prayers and witness of a revived church fellowship it permeates every aspect of life, and, consequently, every value system in that community becomes subservient to this profound presence of God. This is the consistent testimony of every community highlighted on the *Transformations* videos produced by the Sentinel Group. In Cali (Colombia), Almolonga (Guatemala), the Hebrides of Scotland, the Eastern Arctic of Canada and the nation of Uganda, the presence of God began to influence and change every part of society—politically, economically, educationally, morally and ethically, ecologically and spiritually. Having experienced the same degree of divine visitation, each of these communities—as well as countless others throughout the world—continues this process of being changed from one degree of glory to another. It is highly unlikely we will ever find a perfect community this side of the New Jerusalem, before the return of Jesus Christ. At the same time, if revival is stewarded correctly, then transformation should be observable on an ever-changing basis at every level of life. Such transformation becomes part of the divine process as the Lord releases His presence and His glory among His people.

Recently I read an e-mail message from a Christian worker in Uganda. He was asked to describe the revival and transformation that is currently taking place in his nation. He replied that he was not aware of any particular degree of transformation taking place that was different from normal life. He went on to say that regularly people are being saved, healed and delivered, that the economy is continuing to change and that there is a new level of ethics and morality within the political and business spheres of life. He said, "This is now a regular way of life for us. If that is what you mean by transformation, then it is occurring every day . . . but why should this be unusual?" In other words, this man has become used to having the presence of God at work in normal day-to-day life in Uganda!

Duncan Campbell recounted an occasion during the revival in the Hebrides when he and thirty other people met in a cottage following a time of passionate prayer and waiting on the Lord. Suddenly, amazing things began to take place. He described the presence of God coming upon the community in this way: " . . . the house shook like a leaf, the dishes rattled on the sideboard, and an elder standing beside me said, 'Mr. Campbell, an earth tremor.' I said, 'Yes,' and I pronounced the benediction immediately and walked out to find the community alive with an awareness of God."[15]

Referring to this same incident, Kathie Walters, in her book *Bright and Shining Revival,* cites various examples in which people all over the island were searching for God:

Lights were burning in the homes along the road . . . three men were found [lying] by the roadside in a torrent of conviction, crying out for God to have mercy on them . . . seven men were being driven to the meeting in a butcher's truck when suddenly the Spirit of God fell on them in great conviction, and all were saved before they reached the church building . . . outside the police station a crowd of people gathered, weeping and in great distress . . . men and women were kneeling everywhere by the roadside, outside the cottages, even behind the peat stacks, praying for God to have mercy on them.[16]

She later described how this supernatural manifestation of God began to express itself throughout the islands:

So overwhelming sometimes was the Presence of God that people were afraid to open their mouths lest they utter words that would bring judgment upon themselves. People walked quietly before God and, as in every true revival, many a shop became a pulpit, many a home a sanctuary, and many a heart became an altar.[17]

Two Historic Examples of Revival and Transformation

We could examine numerous examples of historical revival and its subsequent transformation, such as the well-known First and Second Great Awakenings in the 1700s and early 1800s or the Baby Boomer Revival from 1965–71, but I have selected only two in order to look at the similarities in two very different cultures. Then we will briefly review some examples in more contemporary settings.

Revival and Transformation in Wales

In the winter of 1904–5 a great religious revival began to develop in Wales under the ministry of such people as the Reverend Evan Roberts (1878–1951). At the conclusion of that revival, more than one hundred thousand conversions were recorded. Desmond Cartwright, the official historian of the Elim Pentecostal churches, refers to the fact that there was widespread coverage of the Welsh Revival in both the secular and Christian press during those months.[18] This is important for us to note because when genuine transformation takes place within a community or a region, it always attracts the attention of the media.

Quoting the Reverend Owen Murphy in his publication *When God Stepped Down from Heaven*, Kathie Walters refers to this description of the Welsh Revival:

This is revival! When men in the streets are afraid to open their mouths and utter godless words lest the judgment of God should fall; when sinners, overawed by the presence of God, tremble in the street and cry for mercy; when, without special meetings and sensational advertising, the Holy Ghost sweeps across cities and towns in supernatural power and holds men in the grip of terrifying conviction; when every shop becomes a pulpit; every heart an altar; every home a sanctuary and people walk softly before God—this is revival! . . . The Welsh revival of 1904 was like a mighty tornado. The Spirit of God swept across the land until mountains and valleys, cities and villages were filled with the mighty manifestations of God. Churches were crowded and meetings went on day and night. Prayer, singing and testimonies would sweep over congregations in torrents, and hundreds turned to Christ. Never in the history of Wales had such indescribable scenes been witnessed.[19]

As I mentioned above, even the secular press gave extraordinary descriptions of the revival as it began to transform communities within Wales. When undertaking some personal research concerning the Welsh Revival, I visited the *Western Mail* newspaper headquarters in Cardiff, Wales. As I went through its archives on the Welsh Revival, I was fascinated to discover how Evan Roberts had used the secular press to his advantage in order to bring glory to God! This newspaper reported the living God in action.

In their book *The Ten Greatest Revivals Ever*, Elmer Towns and Douglas Porter quote historian J. Edwin Orr concerning the impact of the Welsh Revival on the wider culture:

> Drunkenness was immediately cut in half, and many taverns went bankrupt. Crime was so diminished that judges were presented with white gloves signifying that there were no cases of murder, assault, rape or robbery or the like to consider. The police became unemployed in many districts. Stoppages occurred in coal mines, not due to unpleasantness between management and workers, but because so many foul-mouthed miners became converted and stopped using foul language that the horses which hauled the coal trucks in the mines could no longer understand what was being said to them.[20]

At one stage Dr. Campbell Morgan of Westminster Chapel in London traveled to Wales to authenticate the extraordinary stories of transformation that were coming from that area. He declared,

> Here is revival that comes from heaven. . . . Wales is ablaze for God, already 50,000 converts have been recorded and the great awakening shows no signs of waning. It is sweeping over hundreds of villages and cities, emptying saloons, theaters and dance halls and filling the churches night after night with praying multitudes. Go where you will: into the bank; the store; the trains. Everywhere men are talking about God.[21]

In *When God Stepped Down from Heaven*, the Reverend Owen Murphy highlights the significance of this transformation in Wales:

> Like a tree shaken by a mighty storm, Wales was moved by the power of God until almost every home in the nation felt its impact. Newspapers in bold headlines carried the news of the amazing scenes taking place. So great was the fear of God, and conviction gripped the people, that in some communities crime disappeared. . . . In more than one place the post office's supply of money orders were exhausted as people sought to make restitution by paying their debts. Saloons and theaters were closed and stores were sold out of Bibles and New Testaments. Members of Parliament, busy attending revival services, postponed their political meetings. Theatrical companies coming into districts found no audience, for all the world was praying.[22]

While not all revivals that have taken place historically can bear witness to such extraordinary transforming power in the life of a community, the Welsh Revival indicates a degree to which the presence of God can permeate and change every level of society. J. Edwin Orr describes the Welsh Revival as "the farthest reaching of the moments of general awakening. . . . [V]isiting pastors from Norway, Japan, America, India, South Africa and Korea all were deeply moved by the Welsh Revival and became carriers of revival to their nations as they returned home."[23]

Revival and Transformation in Korea

Korea experienced a series of revivals early in the twentieth century that changed the Korean church. Many of the missionaries in the nation were deeply moved by the accounts of revival that had been taking place in Wales. In the early days of January 1907, leaders representing hundreds of churches began to pray together and wait upon the Lord, and the power of God did indeed descend upon the people. Although fear came upon many people initially, this particular revival had a significant impact upon the communities that the churches were attempting to reach. "As the churches were revived, they were gripped by a burning passion to reach the lost in their community. Everywhere, revived churches began to see drunkards, gamblers, adulterers, murderers, thieves, self-righteous . . . transformed into new creatures in Christ."[24] The effect of this revival was carried into many village churches throughout Korea, and to this day the seeds of that revival provide a feeding trough for many of the large churches within South Korea.

Current Examples of Revival and Transformation

Examining revivals that have taken place over the last several hundred years, it is often not difficult to trace the extent to which the revival began to transform the entire community and beyond. Let us take a closer look at some of the various communities highlighted in the *Transformations* videos produced by the Sentinel Group.

Changes in Cali, Colombia

In Cali, Colombia, the situation is far from perfect due to the presence of guerilla groups, and continuing threats against the government, local mayors and certain pastors. However, as the transforming power of God touched that city, corruption was exposed at many levels and drug lords began to be removed. Ruth Ruibal, who has ministered in Cali for many years, along with her husband, Julio, prior to his assassination, says that the situation in Cali continues to improve. Even though there is much work still to be done, she says there is simply no comparison to the way Cali used to be.[25] It is a matter of perspective—deciding if the glass is half empty or half full!

Revival in Guatemala

The community of Almolonga, Guatemala, is also highlighted on the first *Transformations* video. Every aspect of life in Almolonga was dramatically altered as the city's church fellowships stewarded the presence of God with wisdom and prayer. Several other Guatemalan communities indicate even more advanced transformation than is occurring in Almolonga, which is now known around the world for its large carrots! In the mid–1970s about 2 percent of the citizens of Guatemala were born-again Christians. That number is now approximately 47 percent.[26] In many parts of Guatemala, including Guatemala City, the presence of God is beginning to permeate every part of society. The Guatemalan people are learning how to steward the presence of God in such a manner that the glory of God's presence will be reflected at every level of life.

Revival in the Arctic

The new territory of Nunavut and the northern homeland of Nunavik in the eastern Arctic of Canada are highlighted on the second *Transformations* video. In such communities as Pond Inlet, the power and presence of God has descended with extraordinary passion and urgency. In Pond Inlet and other northern communities, the social ills of wife and child abuse, suicide, drug abuse, alcoholism and general despair and despondency have turned around to such an extent that these communities have now become an expression and example of what the larger cities in southern Canada long to experience. Even as I write these words, this move of God continues right across the Canadian Arctic.

Revival in Uganda

For many decades Uganda has handed down a legacy of utter dishevelment at every level. The nation was subjected to an extended season of utter chaos and crisis during the leadership days of Idi Amin and Milton Obote. Dreadful atrocities took place under the government of these men. Then Uganda became the victim of the AIDS crisis. It was not until the leadership of the Church in Uganda began to call out to God with desperation and passion that things began to change quite dramatically. Although life is far from perfect in that nation, life has begun to change to such an extent that the obvious level of transformation confounds other nations in the world. Even in the political arena, a new governmental post for the Minister of Ethics and Integrity was established. This person's responsibility is to remove all corruption from Ugandan society.

Life in Uganda has taken on new meaning in every direction—in politics, the economy, the areas of health and education, and the Church itself. A profound depth of unity has developed among pastors in the city of Kampala. Throughout the country a new church or ministry begins almost daily. On January 1, 2000, an extraordinary covenant was read to thousands gathered at Mandela National Stadium. With the agreement of the president and his wife, church leaders read the document, in which the entire nation of Uganda was given in covenant back to God under the lordship of Jesus Christ for the next one thousand years. On behalf of the nation, the leadership asked forgiveness for all forms of idolatrous worship, untimely bloodshed and broken covenants on the parts of themselves and their ancestors. They then pledged themselves to be a nation that would stand for godly values, renouncing racial and tribal discrimination. They asked God to bless and prosper their nation, including all their national programs in the fields of education, health, agriculture, industry, the roads and communications infrastructure, poverty eradication and the establishment of understanding among differing social groups.

This is the type of declaration that will undoubtedly attract God's attention. The nation of Uganda has chosen to be used by the Lord for His purposes among the other nations of the world. Revival is at work in a profound way in the life of that land, and the work of God's transforming power is being reflected at all levels of national life on an ever-increasing basis. As the leaders of that nation choose to steward the purposes and presence of God in their midst, Uganda will surely enter into its destiny, part of which is defined in its call as "The Pearl of Africa."

Revival in Fiji

Some years ago my wife and I had the privilege of spending time in Fiji and ministering briefly in several local villages. We were touched and blessed by the wonderful gentleness of these people. At the same time, we were disturbed by the obvious degree of poverty in areas not immediately seen by the tourists. In May 2000, the nation was drawn into chaos when a military coup took place under the rogue politician George Speight. The nation was in crisis.

In response, many pastors and their congregations became convicted of their prayerlessness and lack of unity. As they began to draw together in prayer and repentance, the Association of Christian Churches in Fiji (ACCF) was formed. This organization began to facilitate many meaningful transformation partnerships throughout the Body of Christ, as well as in other areas of national life such as the political arena. Many seeds of faithful ministry were planted in Fiji involving local churches and ministry organizations such as World Vision, Youth With A Mission and Every Home For Christ, to name but a few. These seeds grew quickly and blossomed with a new sense of optimism.

In July 2001, Christians across the nation entered into a season of joint prayer and Bible teaching. On one occasion several thousand people gathered in Albert Park to hear senior church and political leaders welcome the presence of the Lord Jesus to their land. Prime Minister Laisenia Qarase apologized publicly for the nation's dreadful treatment of many of its inhabitants. This paved the way for national reconciliation. Several Christians were then voted into strategic government positions. A hunger for God is developing in political and economic arenas. Similar to the situation in Uganda, political leaders—including the prime minister and the president—began to intercede for their land. Even George Speight, Fijian nationalist and coup leader, came to Christ in prison along with many of his fellow conspirators.

Encouraged by many of their leaders, the people of Fiji have begun to enter into a lifestyle that reflects the purposes of Jesus Christ. Behind the scenes, the intercessors of the local churches continue to seek the Lord's direction and favor upon their country. Fiji has begun to experience a change in the quality of its agriculture, one of the seven blessings of God to which I refer in my book *Releasing Heaven on Earth*. Ecological change takes place when the people of God seek His face, turn from their wicked ways, and ask Him to heal their land (see 2 Chronicles 7:14).[27]

Other changes developing within Fiji include a recovering economy, a lowering crime rate and a developing Christian media, including a Christian newspaper, radio station and television station. Even though much must still be addressed, Fiji is a nation that is now beginning to experience God's transforming power. As is the case with many other historical revivals, this transformation is what takes place when revival goes beyond the church walls into the heart of the community.

Revival Is Just Around the Corner

The last seven years bear testimony to the fact that the world is experiencing an increase of pressure at virtually every level of life—politically, economically, socially, ethically, morally and spiritually. The events of September 11, 2001, seem to have conditioned people toward an expectation of increasing turmoil and unrest. At the same time, the Christian Church is experiencing an ever-increasing explosion of life on a worldwide basis.

In fact, some missiologists say that what is presently taking place is unprecedented in terms of Church history. Africa, often referred to as the Dark Continent, is now reflecting rays of heavenly light in many areas. The May 2002 issue of *Charisma* magazine refers to the fact that some Christian missiologists believe Nigeria is 45 percent Christian, while others believe the statistic is closer to 60 percent.[28] Other African nations such as Benin and Liberia report major changes as well, influenced by a spiritual change in the leadership of such nations. Similar reports are received from a number of nations in South America, as well as in regions of the Ukraine and Russia, in which large numbers of people are coming to Christ.

Seemingly, many nations in the world are being positioned for national revival that will usher in the "Great Harvest" that many believe will occur in the years preceding the return of Christ. Even in North America, the term *revival* is on the lips of many leaders, giving the impression that a defining move of God is literally just around the corner! We are being challenged in the Church today to rethink the deeper implication of Matthew 28:19–20. It is as if entire nations are being positioned by the Lord to enter into their respective destinies and become models of ministry to other nations, discipling such nations in the purposes of the Lord.

If God is indeed positioning His Church for a dramatic move of the Holy Spirit on a worldwide basis in these stretching days, then we are challenged by the searching question: *Can revival be stewarded in order to release authentic transformation and lasting change within society?* The remaining chapters of this book are devoted to responding to this question.

Exploring such a question does not portend taking a position for a "dominion theology." If anything, Scripture implies an increasing intensity in the extent of evil in society prior to the return of Christ. However, Scripture also directs us to remain busy fulfilling the work of the Kingdom of God on a day-to-day basis until the Lord returns. As God's prophetic voice in society, the Christian Church must continue the ongoing business of changing the spiritual and moral condition of the world until the Lord comes for His Bride. My personal passion is for the witness of the Church to have an impact on all levels of society today in such a way that Jesus' invitation becomes irresistible, reflecting and releasing the purposes of God upon and within the individual, the city and the nation. The challenge is this: When the Lord enters our midst, can His presence be sustained in order for His glory to be released? Can we steward revival so that it becomes an ongoing transformation of society at all levels, and so that we may become a resting place for the glory of God? Our journey will provide answers to these searching questions.

2

...

Can We Steward the Presence of the Lord?

Bear up the hands that hang down, by faith and prayer; support the tottering knees. Have you any days of fasting and prayer? Storm the throne of grace and persevere therein, and mercy will come down.

John Wesley

In his book *Informed Intercession,* George Otis Jr. makes an interesting comment: "The ideal is that spiritual transformation remains a permanent condition. Unfortunately, history shows that the blossom of revival (to use a loose definition of the term) lasts an average of 36 months." Otis attaches a footnote to this comment saying that this is the time estimate derived from Dr. C. Peter Wagner of the Wagner Leadership Institute, formerly Professor of Church Growth at Fuller Theological Seminary. He continues on this theme by saying, "Exceptions exist— the Argentine Revival has lingered more than fifteen years—but these are few and far between."[1] Since Otis penned those words, this revival has continued to influence both Argentina and other nations—now extending beyond twenty years.

Roy Fish, a contributing author of *Revival!*, believes that revival is "new life," and that while God is the giver of life, "as a rule, God does not work independently on people. This is true both in securing and sustaining revival."[2] Fish goes on to say that he believes revival can be sustained for many years, and that even when the general nature comes to an end, "local churches can continue to live in the experience of awakening" (p.152). Fish also supports Luther's belief that revival could last thirty years, while Wesley said forty years.[3] Yet, a brief glance around most of society today tells us this is rarely the case. Why?

In 1969 Gerald Fry accepted a pastorate in the area of San Jose, California, now known as the Silicon Valley. In his book *In Pursuit of His Glory,* Fry recounts the extraordinary move of God in that area: "Throughout the decade of the '70s, God established in us several foundational truths, all the while fashioning a people who could be the receptacles of His glory, a people who could *steward revival*" (emphasis mine).[4] In 1982 a divine visitation took place that released revival upon the local church. Fry goes on to say that they faithfully followed certain principles that God apparently honored. They resolved to go where they sensed the life of the Spirit. They resolved not to control the visitation of God. They sought prophetic counsel and followed the five–fold ministry outline of Ephesians 4. They sought to balance evangelism with systematic teaching of the Word of God, and they became aware of the ways in which this divine visitation was affecting other areas of the city.[5] This divine visitation from God, this revival, released the Word of God over and around and upon His people. Up to four thousand people became part of this thriving church fellowship.

The church, however, does not exist today. What happened? Gerald Fry knew the importance of stewarding this revival, yet issues developed that eventually eroded and weakened the work God had begun in the midst of His people.

The object of this book is to look carefully at the subject of stewarding the presence and the effect of revival and to explore how such stewardship is intimately tied to the profound presence and pleasure of God coming to rest upon and within the midst of His people. As we have already seen, He longs to have His glory among us. Yet, why is it that so many examples of historical revival ended within a 36–month period (a comment also made by Charles Finney)? And why is it that in so many cases of revival traceable throughout the pages of history, the presence of God never had a transforming effect within the local community, at least on a measurable basis?

In my involvement within the Church at large, I visit many local churches in various parts of the world. In certain cases, churches have experienced authentic revival, but it is hard to recognize that fact judging from the state of the communities in which they exist. The purpose of the Kingdom of God coming upon the kingdom of man is to impact the kingdom of man in such a way that God's will is done on earth as it is in heaven! If a community does not change in many ways—including spiritually—as a result of revival happening in local churches, then it means that the Church and community are not in relation with each other!

In *Releasing Heaven on Earth*, I begin to address this question in chapters 7, 8 and 9. As I understand Scripture, becoming a steward of the land and the city is among the highest of callings that God gives to His people here on earth. According to what we read in Scripture, we are in fact looking after God's own property, and He expects us to extend His authority, glory and presence to the ends of the earth. I believe that this is intimately tied to the way we "occupy" the territory God has assigned to us and that "whatever we *attain* for Christ, we must *maintain* in order to *retain* it."[6] In this book, my objective is to explore what I mentioned in *Releasing Heaven on Earth*: how we maintain and retain God's presence in our midst.

I believe God is calling His Church into an extraordinary season of preparation for a divine visitation on a scale that goes beyond our comprehension. However, God also expects us to steward this coming revival so that His transforming power can impact every aspect of society with lasting results. I appreciate what Gerald Fry says: "The great secret to *'stewarding revival'* (emphasis mine) is 'to act justly, and to love mercy and to walk humbly with your God' (Micah 6:8)."[7] It is also interesting to note that the next verse, Micah 6:9, reads: "Listen! The Lord is calling to the city. . . ." It is my passionate belief that God wants entire cities to come under the influence and joy of His transforming power, and revival can be stewarded in order to release authentic transformation and allow the presence and the glory of God to be made manifest. However, before we continue our in-depth study of this issue that is so close to God's heart, let us look briefly at some of the historic and biblical reasons for the loss of revival.

Historic and Biblical Reasons for the Loss of Revival

In chapter four of his book, Fry gives a very honest and open account of what went wrong in their fellowship during the eventide period of that revival. He cites a number of reasons why revival comes to an end—reasons that many leaders have given throughout the ages of the Church. Perhaps the revival served its purpose and its ending was a matter of God's timing. Or perhaps pride crept into the leadership—or burnout. Or maybe the revival itself became the focus instead of Jesus. Or divergent doctrinal issues may have developed among members of the leadership. Fry says, "The Pentecostal Awakening at the beginning of this century had its share of feuding, the acrimonious split between two of the 'fathers' of that revival—Charles Parham and Brother Seymour of the Azusa Street Mission—being the most notable."[8] In his book *Seasons of Revival*, Frank Damazio says, "Revival seasons come and go, . . . no spiritual awakening lasts forever—twenty, thirty or forty years, maybe—but the truths discovered and the spiritual life released can be sustained forever."[9] Why is it that "revival seasons" so often "come and go"?

Many church leaders have speculated that Evan Roberts experienced burnout and that this was a reason for the early conclusion of the Welsh Revival. Yet, it is interesting to note that although Roberts was directly involved with the Welsh Revival only for a few months, the effect of that revival had worldwide significance and to this day challenges many people into a deeper walk with the Lord—even if Wales itself at present reveals few real indicators of that significant time!

What exactly did go wrong during these days of revival experienced by Gerald Fry and his people? Fry states his belief that something was compromised. While not having all the answers to what went wrong, he identifies certain factors:

1. *We allowed the excitement of the crowds and the miracles to dull our ears from hearing the whole counsel of God.* In other words, the sheer momentum carried them beyond the boundaries of wise counsel.
2. *Personally, I was looking at all the excitement and the crowds as a means of shoring up some weaknesses in our own home fellowship.* He admits a subtle motivation of fear and

so was not always attuned to the voice of God in every detail of stewarding the visitation.

3. *We let a very subtle attitude of pride and showmanship emerge in the way we promoted the vision.* Pride became a factor, and they knew they were hosting a move of God!

4. *Unfortunately, we suspended many of the ordinary disciplines of our church life and structure.* They indeed welcomed the presence of the Lord to their corporate fellowship and were aware of the possibility of programming the Holy Spirit. However, this also meant that without the necessary programs ministering to the needs of the people, the pastoral work of the church became an issue of concern.

5. *We did not make the shift to "making disciples."* Having suspended their home group program, they also lost an effective discipleship program.

6. *The authority structure of the revival itself began to weaken.* The leadership did not have correct ministry boundaries, and as a result a structural stress began to develop.

7. *I delegated authority incorrectly.* "Professionals" were hired to look after the needs of the growing congregation, but this was done at the expense of in-house mentoring and the release of up-and-coming ministers from within the fellowship—a definite early Church principle!

8. *One of the greatest mistakes we made was losing our hunger to simply worship God.* Instead of basking in the presence of God through worship, the worship became a means of furthering the revival. Subtle as it may sound, the emphasis of the worship turned to building faith, rather than focusing solely upon God.

9. *Hand in hand with this, we neglected perhaps the most important thing of all—prayer.* Slowly, the "busyness" of the revival became the priority, and their intercessory prayer strategy began to weaken.

10. *We failed to discern that God wanted us to plant churches.*
    They forgot the multiplication mandate as described
    in the book of Acts. Revival is not a matter of extend-
    ing numbers; it is a matter of church planting and
    discipleship.
11. *There was something else we failed to recognize at the time:
    we were the "host church" of this revival.* Part of their call
    was to be the grain of wheat that died in order that
    other church fellowships would blossom.
12. *We neglected to "feed the sheep."* Fry admits he was
    neglecting the needs of the sheep, so complaints and
    criticisms began to develop, opening the door to dis-
    cord and strife.[10]

In all likelihood, if we were to study the "demise" of other
revivals over the centuries, many of the issues cited by Gerald Fry would be observed. Although revival is a miracle of
divine grace and in many cases is God's response to the
heartfelt cry of His people, any form of opposition—both
human and satanic—can hinder revival even before it has
begun. This again is a stewardship issue—an issue that was
very much on the minds of both Jonathan Edwards and
Charles Finney. Let us briefly review what they listed as the
most common hindrances to revival:

1. *The revival will stop when church members believe it is
   going to stop.* When this mindset develops, it is hard
   for any revival to gain momentum.
2. *A revival will cease when Christians consent that it should.*
   If the Body of Christ is not willing to pay the price
   in stewarding revival, they are basically consenting
   that it should come to an end.
3. *A revival will end when Christians become mechanical in
   their attempts to promote it.* Strong faith and infectious
   enthusiasm can promote a revival, but if these are
   not present the revival probably will end.

4. *The revival will cease when Christians embrace the idea that the work will go on without their input.* The Body of Christ is all part of the hands-on process in sharing the Word of God and in demonstrating His purpose within the life of the community.

5. *The work will cease when church members prefer to attend to their own concerns rather than to God's business.* The things of God must always take prominence over the cares of the world. This became most apparent during the days of the Welsh Revival, in which even members of Parliament and magistrates were attending prayer meetings rather than going to their secular employment!

6. *When Christians become proud of a great revival, it will cease.* Pride and the presence of God cannot co-exist.

7. *Revival will stop when the Church becomes overworked.* Even Christians need nourishment and rest in order to continue the work of revival.

8. *A revival will cease when the church begins to speculate about abstract doctrines, which have nothing to do with practice.* The focus of salvation must never be lost.

9. *When Christians begin to proselytize, it is the beginning of the end of God's working in their midst.* Revival will end when denominations start to focus on themselves rather than on the Body of Christ. To be able to defer to each other and to prefer each other is a powerful spiritual principle.

10. *When Christians refuse to render to the Lord according to the benefits they have received, the work of the Spirit will see a cooling down.* When the Lord blesses us, we also need to be an ongoing blessing to others by what we do and through what we give.

11. *When the church in any way grieves the Holy Spirit, He cannot abide with them.* It is important that we do not misjudge or disapprove of the holy things of God, whether wittingly or through ignorance.

12. *A revival may be expected to cease when Christians lose the spirit of brotherly love.* Relational unity is a critical factor in attracting the presence of God into a community.

13. *A revival will decline and cease unless Christians are frequently humbled before God.* Even the mature Christian recognizes that his dependence upon the Lord will never end.

14. *A revival cannot continue when Christians do not practice self-denial.* When self-indulgence replaces self-denial, the Spirit of God in our midst becomes less apparent.

15. *A revival will be stopped by controversies about new measures.* Many a revival has come to an end due to this issue. At this point the Body of Christ needs to be in constant submission to the Holy Spirit and to any direction in which He chooses to guide and direct His people.

16. *Revivals can be put down by the continued opposition of the "old school" combined with a bad spirit in the "new school."* This becomes a flesh-and-blood issue and, rather than being caught up with the Lord, we become more involved in defending human agendas!

17. *Any diversion of the public mind will hinder a revival.* The presence of God—and the presence of God alone—must become our focal point in order for revival to be sustained.

18. *Neglect of the claims of missions is another hindrance to revival.* Similar to what Gerald Fry learned, we need to be concerned with planting new churches and extending the Kingdom of God into new areas.

19. *When a church rejects the call of God upon it for the education of young people for the ministry, it will hinder and destroy a revival.* To the degree that we invest in the youth of society, it is to the same degree that we can expect to see transformation develop within our communities through the life and work of future

leaders. We will be examining this point in some
detail later in this book.

20. *Slandering revivals often will put them down.* When any
local church fellowship slanders or misrepresents the
work of God in another fellowship, it is almost certain that the Holy Spirit will be grieved and revival
will soon wane.

21. *Ecclesiastical difficulties are calculated to grieve the Holy
Spirit and to destroy revivals.* At times denominational
structures and ministry organizations are blind to the
reviving work of God and levy restrictions upon their
people that remove them from the arena of revival.

22. *Another thing by which revivals may be hindered is cen-
soriousness on either side, and especially in those who have
been engaged in carrying forward a revival.* When the
stewards of revival remain humble and in a spirit of
fervent prayer and are not deflected through what
opponents may say against them, revival will continue. Otherwise, being interrupted by such distractions releases the flesh within us and displaces the
work of the Spirit.[11]

Invaluable lessons can be learned through the assess-
ments of Fry, Edwards and Finney. In the pages that follow, we will see that these are, in fact, the very lessons of
stewardship God wants us to understand in advance before
His glory comes upon us. One of these lessons concerns
David's response to the presence of God.

Understanding the Presence of the Lord

First Samuel 4 describes a somber time in the life of
Israel. Due to the sin of God's people—even sin within the
household of Eli—the Ark of the Covenant was removed

from the people of God and handed over to the Philistines. The Ark was positioned in the temple dedicated to the Philistine god Dagon (see 1 Samuel 5:2). It is not possible, however, to mix the holiness of God with the unholiness of a false deity. Scripture says the Philistines became afflicted with tumors, which some Bible teachers refer to as a case of corporate hemorrhoids! Very painful! The Philistines knew it was essential to remove the Ark of the Covenant from their midst and they placed it on a cart pulled by cows to return it to the people of God (see 1 Samuel 6:7–12). However, God knew the Israelites were not yet ready to steward His presence (see 1 Samuel 6:19). Subsequently, the Ark was positioned in the household of Abinadab (see 1 Samuel 7:1).

First Chronicles 13–15 and 2 Samuel 6 describe what happened twenty years later when David sought to return the Ark of the Covenant to Jerusalem. The Ark was placed on a new cart pulled by oxen and guided by Uzzah and Ahio, who were sons of Abinadab. At one point the oxen stumbled. When Uzzah reached out to steady the Ark, God immediately struck him dead. David was angry with God for what had taken place. However, we need to look more carefully at what in fact happened!

Originally God instructed that the Ark of the Covenant was to be carried on the shoulders of the Levites—indicating a position of intimacy, authority and presence upon and within the lives of His people. The sobering lesson here is that we can become *so familiar* with our understanding of God that we begin to lose any sense of the fear of God in our lives.

This was the case with Uzzah and Ahio who, as sons of Abinadab, obviously had been used to having the presence of God in their household for twenty years. Uzzah means "strength"; Ahio was Uzzah's brother. The two were guiding the Ark of the Covenant in their own brotherly strength without recognizing the significance of positioning the presence of the Lord in the way God originally commanded His people. Furthermore, when the oxen stumbled, they did so at the threshing floor. Scripture often refers to the threshing floor as the meeting place between God and man—the place where God threshes out the chaff from the seed of mankind. In the Bible references to oxen are often metaphors used to describe leadership. In addition, the cart had been the means by which the Philistines had chosen to move the presence of God twenty years earlier; God's people utilized the "program" instituted by the Philistines, rather than the guideline originally set by the Lord Himself. As David himself observed in 1 Chronicles 15:13, they had not inquired of the Lord as to the prescribed way in which to bring His presence home.

When David realized his mistake he positioned the Ark of the Lord in the house of Obed-Edom (see 2 Samuel 6:9–11), where it stayed for three months. With the presence of the Lord now in his midst, Obed-Edom and his entire household, along with everything he had, were blessed by the Lord (see 2 Samuel 6:11; 1 Chronicles 13:14). This is always what happens when the presence of God comes to rest in the midst of His people! This is the transforming power of God at work.

In the meantime, David researched what had to be done, and so began the process of preparing a place for the Ark of God (see 1 Chronicles 15:1). Finally, when the Ark of the Covenant was retrieved from the house of Obed-Edom, the Levites carried the Ark with poles on their shoulders, in the manner God had commanded in the days of Moses (see 1 Chronicles 15:15). The first attempted revival had failed because certain guidelines were not in place. This is very reassuring because it indicates that God waits until the correct "spiritual protocol" is in place. An attempted revival can later become an authentic revival once everything is in correct divine order!

Understandably, as the Ark was finally brought into Jerusalem, David and the entire house of Israel ushered the presence of the Lord into the city with shouts, dancing and the sound of trumpets (see 2 Samuel 6:14–16). When all this was done in accordance with God's direction, everything—the music, the worship and the offerings—was without discord and brought honor and glory to the Lord, and He was pleased. Obed-Edom, who had experienced the presence of the Lord in such an intimate way for three months, became a doorkeeper for the Ark (see 1 Chronicles 15:24)! When the Lord is honored by His people and is lifted high with holiness, humility and integrity, He draws all people to Himself.

This is how we must understand the glory of the Lord who longs to rest in the midst of His people. If revival is indeed the full measure of God's presence coming upon His people and awakening and quickening them to His holy purposes, then it is evident why God requires a high measure of stewardship to move and work in the power of His presence. The result brings Him absolute honor and glory.

In his classic work, *Why Revival Tarries*, Leonard Ravenhill is direct concerning the absence or lack of revival:

> [I]f we preachers prepared every sermon with one eye on damned humanity and the other on the judgment seat—then we would have a Holy Ghost revival that would shake this earth and that, in no time at all, would liberate millions of precious souls. . . . [M]en built our churches but do not enter them, print our Bibles but do not read them, talk about God but do not believe Him, speak of Christ but do not trust Him for salvation, sing our hymns and then forget them. How are we going to come out of all this?[12]

Very challenging words! Ravenhill's concerns are the compromise and corruption in the church that leave it unable to preach the Word of God with prophetic urgency or to wrestle in prayer. He believes that revival tarries as a result of commercialism in the life of the church and in some of the evangelists, which in turn leads to a "cheapening of the Gospel"[13] in our manner of worship. Therefore, due to carelessness in church priorities, a fear of man and a lack of urgency in prayer, the integrity and urgency within the church are lost. Furthermore, Ravenhill believes revival does not come since man steals the glory that belongs to God. He says we must "alter the altar."[14]

In recent years I have read several books on the subject of revival. Every author has varying beliefs as to why revivals end, but there is one common denominator. When the intense travailing prayer that attracted God's presence begins to wane, the blessing of revival becomes short-lived. Fish, for example, says, "[T]he conditions for sustaining revival are basically the same. The conditions for beginning a revival are also the conditions for seeing it perpetuated."[15] Therefore, if people cease praying and no longer walk in a relationship of humility, holiness and repentance with God and each other, then revival will end.

Through my personal research on this topic over the last several years, I have isolated ten main areas that may be viewed as "principles of stewardship." When understood and applied in the power of the Holy Spirit, these principles will ensure that His presence will remain in our midst.

As I mentioned in the Introduction, 2 Chronicles 7:14 is a familiar verse to many of us in this day and age: "If my people, who are called by my name, will humble themselves and pray and seek my face and turn from their wicked ways, then will I hear from heaven and will forgive their sin and will heal their land." Again, note carefully those next two verses that indicate the *purpose* of God's coming to dwell in the midst of His people: "Now my eyes will be open and my ears attentive to the prayers offered in this place. I have chosen and consecrated this temple so that my Name may be there forever. My eyes and my heart will always be there" (2 Chronicles 7:15–16). This is extraordinary—the Name of

God (His presence) wanting to dwell among us so that His eyes and ears will be attentive to our needs! This indicates to me that God wants His presence to continue to dwell with us, and this surely is an indicator that He longs to transform His people, His cities and His land so that His presence and His glory are reflected to all the nations of the world.

Taking into account all that we have observed so far concerning historic and contemporary revival and transformation, we will now look at each one of these ten principles of stewardship. Just as preparing a resting place for the Lord became a critical issue of leadership for David, so it is for us today. And stewarding God's presence is critical to preparing a habitation for Him.

3

...

Persevering Leadership

The only saving faith is that which casts itself on God for life or death.

Martin Luther

Looking through the pages of revival history, certain individuals who were used by the Lord in unique ways inevitably catch our attention. For example, Evan Roberts is in many ways synonymous with the Welsh Revival of 1904. A man of great prayer, Roberts was also aggressive and tenacious in his desire to see the purposes of God come to pass at that time. Putting it simply, he was a persevering servant of God!

The testimony of such revivalists as Evan Roberts, Charles Finney and Duncan Campbell reveal this essential spiritual principle that is present in every historic example of authentic revival. Almost without exception, every revival in the history of the Church has occurred when leadership was willing to pay the price. Persevering leaders are essential to the release of God's transforming power, and in order for transformation to follow revival, persevering leaders need to be people of tenacity and aggressiveness who will not quickly let go of the vision God entrusts to them.

In his book *City-Wide Prayer Movements: One Church, Many Congregations,* Tom White refers to his home community of Corvallis. Along with several other leaders from the various congregations of that community, Tom had a vision for a special initiative that took place on Easter in the year 2000. It was clearly an event that had an impact on many people, and God's glory was poured out over Corvallis. But, in White's own words, they hit a "classic plateau": "In the aftermath of victory, the enemy has roamed our city as a roaring, angry lion, and we have had our share of discouragement, warfare and turmoil in several key churches."[1]

White outlines both the strengths and the weaknesses of what has occurred since that citywide church initiative, including a long-term intercessory investment in the community. He goes on to talk about the cycles and seasons in which "the Spirit breathes on our brokenness, renews our desperation and rekindles momentum. So, wise, persevering leaders lay 'tracks' of enduring biblical vision that keep right on going through the highs and lows, the praise gatherings, the outreaches, the death or departure of key leaders and the seasonal strengths and weaknesses of local churches."[2]

This seems to be a critical comment as far as persevering leadership is concerned. A persevering leader is someone who understands the dynamic of fervent prayer that is ingrained in a God-given vision. He becomes both the plumbline and the litmus test for maintaining that vision until it is fulfilled. A persevering leader knows how to *attract* God's presence into a community but also must learn how to *sustain* the presence of the Lord.

Attracting God's Presence

Certain things attracted me to my wife, Marie. Her smile, her features, her big brown eyes, her wisdom and her wonderful personality were but a few of the many characteristics that made her irresistible to me! Similarly, the presence of God is attracted to such factors as holiness, humility and unity. When such elements are present in the Body of Christ, we are irresistible to Him! On the reverse, however, various issues and sins on the land and in our communities can offend the Lord, such as I addressed in *Releasing Heaven on Earth*.[3]

If we want our church, our city or our nation to form a lasting relationship with the Lord where His presence remains in our midst, then we need to dust off the welcome mat and present ourselves as a holy and living sacrifice that is pleasing to God (see Romans 12:1). The persevering leader needs to recognize that certain things must be rectified initially in the life and fellowship of the local church leadership before the Lord will feel comfortable in our midst! He also must be able to demonstrate the qualities that attract the Lord at both a personal and corporate level.

And it will be said: "Build up, build up, prepare the road! Remove the obstacles out of the way of my people." For this is what the high and lofty One says—he who lives forever, whose name is holy: "I live in a high and holy place, but also with him who is contrite and lowly in spirit, to *revive* the spirit of the lowly and to *revive* the heart of the contrite."

Isaiah 57:14–15, emphasis mine

This passage implies the removal of certain obstacles in order for God Himself, who lives in a high and holy place, to choose to dwell with those who are humble and contrite in spirit. As the latter part of verse 15 declares, God wants to revive His people, but the issue of humility and contriteness is clearly essential in His relationship with us. This is not simply a call to the entire Body of Christ; it is also specifically a call to leadership. Leadership needs to be wholehearted in its desire to maintain lasting spiritual refreshment. Leadership can never afford to allow pride, arrogance or independence to get in the way of the Lord if He is being invited into the midst of His people. David knew the importance of walking with an undivided heart in order to retain the fear of the Lord in his life (see Psalm 86:11). When God knows we will do what is necessary to remove offense from our lives and to eliminate its effect upon the land, He promises peace and salvation, and our land will once again yield its harvest (see Psalm 85:8–9, 12).

Living in the Posture of Humility

We know from the life of David that humility becomes an essential ingredient in maintaining a day-to-day relationship with the Lord. Roy Fish is one of the few authors who address the subject of sustaining revival. Concerning this issue of humility, he says,

> If revival is to be sustained, God's people must remain humble before Him; they must continue to be steadfast in prayer; they are to be ever seeking the Lord; and they must live lives characterized by repentance and constantly turning from the wicked way. To a degree, the requirements for securing revival become the requirements for sustaining revival.[4]

Leaders must confess an ongoing dependence upon God's sovereignty and lordship. When a leader begins to depend on his or her own strength, intimacy with the Lord is forfeited for self-adoration. Jesus exemplified the importance of maintaining intimacy and dependency upon the Father at all times: "I do nothing on my own but speak just what the Father has taught me. The one who sent me is with me; he has not left me alone, for I always do what pleases him" (John 8:28–29). In the familiar passage of John 17, Jesus reveals an intimacy with the Father that is based on humility, holiness, accountability, integrity and transparency. These are the ingredients that feed His relationship with the Father, and He fully expects us to exhibit these same characteristics in our relationships with each other and with Him!

Jesus implied that when humility is the basis for our relationships with each other, then the world will know that He was sent by God and that His presence dwells in the midst of His people. This is a reflection of Moses' indication that the presence of the Lord would distinguish him and the Lord's people from all the other people on the face of the earth (see Exodus 33:16). We will talk more about the issue of relational unity later in this book. Persevering leaders need to know, however, that the presence of the Lord will tarry in our midst only on the same terms by which the Father and the Son relate to each other.

Jesus expects no less from us as His people. I love this comment: "My food . . . is to do the will of him who sent me and to finish his work" (John 4:34). If we are to finish the work that the Lord has established for us in these stretching, challenging, exciting days, then we must continue to ensure that our posture of humility, holiness and accountability is maintained both with the Lord and with each other. Only in this way can an honest transparency develop in our fellowship that will prevent the enemy from gaining a foothold of entry. This is the quality of relationship and life that not only attracts the presence of God but also develops the leadership that is required for sustaining His presence in our midst. Putting it simply, humility is synonymous with persevering leadership.

Developing a Persevering Leader

Any sport involves a degree of discipline in order to enjoy a measure of success. I enjoy golf, but it can be a complex game if I do not persevere in spending sufficient time with the golf club and ball! If I do not follow certain basic guidelines, my shortcuts and lack of practice land me into all sorts of trouble, and what should be enjoyable becomes little more than an experience of frustration and misery!

This same principle applies to revival. Perseverance is required on the part of leadership in order to keep God's presence in the midst of a body of believers. Scripture has much to say regarding the term *perseverance*. James puts it this way:

> Consider it pure joy, my brothers, whenever you face trials of many kinds, because you know that the testing of your faith develops perseverance. Perseverance must finish its work so that you may be mature and complete, not lacking anything. . . . Blessed is the man who perseveres under trial, because when he has stood the test, he will receive the crown of life that God has promised to those who love him.
>
> James 1:2–4, 12

These words hold a sense of expectation that if we are going to succeed and mature as Christian leaders, then we must expect to undergo perseverance as part of God's growth formula in our Christian walk. Hebrews says something very similar:

> Therefore, since we are surrounded by such a great cloud of witnesses, let us throw off everything that hinders and the sin that so easily entangles, and let us run with perseverance the race marked out for us. . . . Consider him who endured such opposition from sinful men, so that you will not grow weary and lose heart. . . . God disciplines us for our good, that we may share in his holiness. No discipline seems pleasant at the time, but painful. Later on, however, it produces a harvest of righteousness and peace for those who have been trained by it.
>
> Hebrews 12:1, 3, 10–11

Perseverance requires training in the midst of pressure and challenge. This training achieves endurance and holiness, which in turn produces a harvest of righteousness and peace. Not everyone enjoys the process of training. It is hard work—but well worth it according to Hebrews 12.

Revival is usually preceded by a season of exceptional travailing prayer, the confession of sins both individually and corporately, and the tenacity of a number of people in ensuring that the presence of the Lord is made welcome in that place. What occurs in the physical, natural realm is a reflection of what is going on in the invisible, spiritual realm. While this may be a difficult concept for many people—notably those who minister in the Western church and who may not recognize the reality of the spiritual realm—it is nonetheless a reality as far as Scripture is concerned! As we engage with issues on the land, we also are dealing with spiritual issues. Dealing with principalities and powers (see Ephesians 6:12) often means that we are dealing with strongholds and mindsets that can shape the corporate thinking of an entire city—and even a nation. Harold Caballeros refers to this as the "culture of the social conglomerate."[5]

Inevitably, leadership will face not only physical but spiritual issues that can prevent the presence of the Lord from remaining. The persevering leader must be willing to withstand all types of issues that undoubtedly will come his way. The moment the Kingdom of God is engaged in a leader's territory, an inevitable conflict ensues until the spiritual realm and the physical realm are in submission to the higher purposes of Christ. The leader's own life becomes a potential battleground. Hidden agendas, jealousies, lusts of the flesh and relational issues with family and colleagues are just a few of the areas in which the leader will be called upon to persevere.

When a persevering leader deals with the issues of the land, it is normal then that the most vulnerable areas in his personal life suddenly will become exposed or challenged. I refer to such areas of vulnerability as the "spiritual Achilles heel" that so often provides subtle leverage to the enemy of God's people, the one who loves to accuse on a day and night basis when given the opportunity (see Revelation 12:10)! To address a vulnerable area in one's life is rarely pleasant, but it is essential for our ongoing growth as leaders. Authority is determined by the quality of integrity and the stature of one's life in Christ.

In declaring the Good News of the Kingdom of God, Jesus was misunderstood by the law of the land, the Pharisees, the Sadducees, the church of the day, and at times by His own family and His own disciples. Yet, He had utter dependence upon and trust in the Father, and by being in the presence of His Father on numerous occasions, Jesus received what was necessary to handle each situation that confronted Him. This same perseverance in seeking God's presence is essential to church leadership, for they must learn to walk in accountability and integrity with both family and colleagues, as well as with the Lord Himself. This training becomes a discipline that releases supernatural faith in the midst of challenge and controversy.

Ezra: Opposition to Beginning the Work

In revival, God is faithfully and patiently building His Church into a Temple of living stones that will reveal His glory to the rest of the world. Several leaders in the Bible were faced with building programs that were metaphors for the building and construction God wants to develop in our personal and corporate lives. The book of Ezra, for example, records the story of rebuilding the Temple, an act that resulted in fierce opposition from the enemies of the Jews. Haggai and Zechariah were the two prophets appointed to exhort the people to complete their task in spite of the difficulties. Opposition is a key challenge that so often faces the persevering leader.

In his book *Rekindled Flame,* Steve Fry points out that opposition to this particular project began when the building started—not earlier, when the foundations were laid.[6] (We will talk more about foundations in the next chapter on prevailing prayer.) In other words, preserving revival at an early stage includes knowing specifically what areas of relationship-building and vision-building the enemy will target. This is a key role for the persevering leader. Fry also points out that opposition is broken by obedience. As he puts it, "[S]omething of an atomic reaction is unleashed in one simple act of obedience, a reaction that can eventually affect thousands."[7] Obedience is required on the part of the leadership, and the persevering leader will hold the church accountable to the standard of obedience.

A third point Fry makes is that we often "retreat to the safety of our own worlds when 'building the temple' gets too hard."[8] To build the house of the Lord takes hard work—but it requires working together since God chose to reveal the glory of His presence through His people, each of whom reflects something of that glory. We will look later at this whole subject of relational unity, but it is important to recognize here that a challenge to the persevering leader is to see that the church works together in "building the temple."

Receiving God's glory cannot be done with the "instant hamburger" mentality that is so much a part of our daily culture today. I have often seen people push elevator buttons repeatedly, assuming that the initial press of the button was not enough. In reality, the light for the particular floor was already on and the elevator was responding—simply not at the speed desired! Laws of physics, electricity and gravity were at work. The Body of Christ needs to learn similar spiritual laws—otherwise, we become dissatisfied and disappointed. We feel as though the world is against us, God has forgotten about us and we may as well give up. This presents another challenge for the persevering leader: the need for tenacity. The leadership must be truly tenacious in encouraging the church to remain rooted in the spiritual laws God has set and not to become too eager or dissatisfied, thus misunderstanding the timing of God. This is crucial if we want to steward God's presence when He responds to our invitation. As Fry says, "God's rebuke was so severe because He saw that His people were in danger of missing their destiny."[9]

Nehemiah: Opposition to Completing the Work

Nehemiah is one of my favorite examples of a persevering leader who withstood a number of challenges that still face the leaders of today. Nehemiah had to address *personal, private* and *prophetic* pressure in order to protect the work God had called him to undertake.

In the early chapters of the Book of Nehemiah we see how he persevered in his call to get to Jerusalem and repair the walls that had been destroyed. In exile in Babylon, Nehemiah served as cupbearer to King Artaxerxes. One evening, the king asked Nehemiah what lay behind his sadness of heart. Although he feared doing so, Nehemiah was honest and forthright in the face of this authority:

> I was very much afraid, but I said to the king, "May the king live forever! Why should my face not look sad when the city where my fathers are buried lies in ruins, and its gates have been destroyed by fire?" . . . And because the gracious hand of my God was upon me, the king granted my requests.
>
> Nehemiah 2:2–3, 8

Nehemiah's first challenge was to maintain integrity, honesty and forthrightness even in the midst of trepidation.

But Nehemiah's challenges had just begun. When he arrived in Jerusalem he saw for the first time the extent of the destruction. He proceeded to draw up his blueprints, but then he was faced with the three challenges that oppose every persevering leader today.

First of all, Nehemiah was faced with *private* pressure. Several times he received a message from Sanballat and Geshem asking him to meet with them in one of the villages on the plain of Omo. Privately, people were trying to distract him from the initiative at hand. He knew that they were scheming to harm him, and he would not be budged from his responsibilities. As a persevering leader, Nehemiah continually identified his work with the Lord's work and purpose. Therefore, whoever was his enemy and against the work at hand was also the enemy of the Lord.

The second type of pressure experienced by Nehemiah was *public* pressure. This came in the form of the same message sent a fifth time by Sanballat's aide. In Nehemiah 6:5–9, we read how Nehemiah was given an unsealed letter, implying that the letter could well have been read by many people. The contents of the letter suggested that Nehemiah was involved in a rebellion to overthrow the leadership of the land and to set himself up as king. This type of negative report would be enough to distract most leaders in the church today from their responsibilities. Instead, Nehemiah basically said that this accusation was quite false and asked the Lord Himself to strengthen his hands. In other words, he would not give the time of day to such utter nonsense. In responding this way Nehemiah did not allow negativity and lies to be sown into his mind and heart, which in turn would cause him to react and to remove his attention from the work to which God called him. He did not allow himself to be sidetracked by worrying over what other people were saying.

If these first two types of pressure are not successful, the enemy invariably tries a third measure of attack known as *prophetic* pressure. Shemaiah was hired by Tobiah and Sanballat to intimidate Nehemiah by prophesying against him in the work he was trying to complete (see verses 12–13). Nehemiah was told that people were coming to kill him—a not-so-subtle form of intimidation! What made it worse was that it was coming from the lips of a prophet, and verse 14 implies that other prophets were also trying to intimidate him and remove him from the task at hand. Since Nehemiah operated from a base of integrity and honesty, one that would not give in to intimidation and lies, he was able to persevere and overcome the vulnerabilities that were unique to that particular situation. In Nehemiah 6:16 we read that when the enemies of Nehemiah heard what took place, even the surrounding nations were afraid and lost their self-confidence because they recognized that God had been at work in and through Nehemiah.

Such is the degree and depth of vindication and authority that God releases in and through the lives of leaders who are obedient to Him and are willing to do what is required to finish the work. In my own experience it is almost always at the point of breakthrough that the most severe—and sometimes most subtle—forms of challenge will come. The persevering leader needs to be aware of this in advance and at all times remain focused on the Lord and His council.

As Nehemiah faced—and overcame—this enormous pressure to abandon the work, he modeled three characteristics that are critical for every persevering leader. First of all, Nehemiah was a *protector* of God's vision. At all times Nehemiah stayed faithful to the Word of God as well as to the witness of God in his life. He kept the truth of God's Word active in his own life and as a testimony to those who would try to remove him from his God-given mandate.

Nehemiah was also a *projector* of the vision given to him by the Lord. Without fear or compromise either in the presence of the king or later in the presence of those who would oppose him, Nehemiah spoke out with boldness and courage as he projected the purpose of God in rebuilding the walls. As Nehemiah 6:16 says so clearly, "When all our enemies heard about this, all the surrounding nations were afraid and lost their self-confidence, because they realized that this work had been done with the help of our God." Due to Nehemiah's honesty, humility and integrity, God was able to use his persevering character and at the same time project His higher purposes through what Nehemiah accomplished.

Finally, Nehemiah was a *promoter* of God's higher purposes. He always positioned God's purposes higher than the attention he received from those who were scheming and plotting against him. Notice his response to the scheming of Sanballat and Geshem: "I sent messengers to them with this reply: 'I am carrying on a great project and cannot go down. Why should the work stop while I leave it and go down to you?' Four times they sent me the same message, and each time I gave them the same answer" (Nehemiah 6:3–4). At all times Nehemiah positioned God on a higher level of authority than the challenges and intimidation of those opposing the work. This is essential for persevering leaders today as they accept the mandate of welcoming the presence of the Lord onto their land and completing the project once it has begun!

Standing in the Council of the Lord

The people in the days of both Ezra and Nehemiah had to understand what was involved in responding to the council of the Lord—and not to the intimidation of man.

> But which of them has stood in the council of the LORD to see or to hear his word? Who has listened and heard his word? . . . But if they had stood in my council, they would have proclaimed my words to my people and would have turned them from their evil ways and from their evil deeds.
>
> Jeremiah 23:18, 22

What does it mean to stand in the council of the Lord? It means to have eyes and ears that are willing to watch and listen to what the Lord calls us to do in spite of the opinion of man. Standing in His *council* means that we then receive His *counsel*, allowing us to speak forth His word and to execute His vision with authority and accuracy.

A persevering leader is one who speaks forth the word of God even in the face of adversity and challenge. A persevering leader is one who will not give in to the temptation and distraction that often come from people who want to make him their king! A persevering leader is one who will not give in to any form of usury, idolatry, intimidation, indeed anything that is less than the higher purposes that the Lord has in store for His people and for His land. The more a persevering leader engages with the issues of the land, the more likely the threats and challenges that will attempt to remove him from his place of appointing and anointing. This is why those in leadership must develop intimacy with the Lord in order to recognize His call in the midst of clamor all around them.

Persevering Leadership in the Church Today

The Church in the twenty-first century is facing many obstacles to its God-given commission. Indeed, the Church is under an endless challenge to compromise the Word of God as revealed in the life and work of Jesus Christ. Too often today the Church gives in to the pressure of relativism and justification in which society no longer accepts the relevance of the Word of God. Recently, for example, the United States faced a legal challenge to the word *God* in its Pledge of Allegiance, although the case is still pending at the time of this writing. This situation caused an uproar of disbelief within many churches throughout the nation. It is this type of compromise—among many others—against which the leaders of the Church in the United States must take a bold and persevering stand.

A pedigree of perseverance must lie within the life of the person who wants to make a difference for the Kingdom of God in this world. No matter what challenges and distractions come our way, at all times we need to heed the words of 1 John 4:4: "The one who is in you is greater than the one who is in the world."

4

...

Prevailing Prayer

Whole days and weeks have I spent prostrate on the
ground in silent or vocal prayer.

George Whitfield

In addition to persevering leaders, one of the common
denominators found in all historic examples of revival is
the existence of pulsating, prevailing prayer. I appreciate the comment made by C. Peter Wagner concerning the
late Edwin Orr, who was one of the foremost historians
and advocates of revival in the last century. Quoting Orr,
Wagner says, "Whenever God gets ready to do a great
work, He always sets His people a-praying."[1] Wagner cites
the recent examples of Brownsville Assembly of God in
Pensacola, Florida, and the Toronto Airport Christian Fellowship. Both churches prayed fervently for revival over
a season of time, although it is probably more accurate to

suggest that they experienced "renewal" rather than revival.[2] This is also a key component of the nations in revival mentioned earlier from the Sentinel Group's *Transformations* videos—from the Arctic to Nigeria to Guatemala, persistent, prevailing prayer is evident in every case. Other present-day examples all report this one essential ingredient for preparing a community, a city and a nation for the reviving presence of the Lord.

Wagner makes the comment that "revivals are relatively short-lived"[3] and "possibly God has not allowed previous revivals to be extended."[4] But as I already mentioned in chapter 1, it is my belief that God does not want to visit His people on a short-term basis! Wagner does make a distinction between revival *fire* and *afterglow*, the fruit that comes from revival. Granted, a number of revivals in recent history were short-lived. For example, the Great Awakening in the American colonies lasted approximately two years, the Second Great Awakening approximately three years and the Third Great Awakening of 1857–1858 only nine months, which was basically the same length of time as the famous Welsh Revival in 1904–1905. Yet, the Welsh Revival spawned other significant moves of God such as the Korean Revival of 1907. The Argentinean Revival, as I mentioned earlier, is now well beyond its twentieth year, and in spite of certain internal stewardship issues that have arisen from time to time, it has had significant effect upon the life of the Church worldwide. Why is this the case? Does prayer really affect the outcome of revival? In this chapter we will explore the effect that prevailing prayer has on moving revival toward transformation.

You may recall that Charles Finney offered a number of reasons why the revivals during his days lost their sense of intimacy and immediacy with God within 24 to 36 months. He stated specifically that when people stopped praying with the same level of expectancy and determination that they had prior to revival, the revivals began to dissolve and disappear. In many cases the communities returned to the condition in which they had been before the presence of the Lord came into their midst.

It is also interesting to note that the character of people in Latin America, Africa and the eastern Arctic—where revival is currently thriving—lends itself to the discipline of regular and lasting prayer much more regularly than that of the Church in the Western world. Thus, it appears that the type of prayer that ignites revival has a determining effect upon the length and depth of the revival. Putting it another way, *revival can really be sustained only if the necessary prayer is active and can handle the increasing responsibility of sustaining a revival.*

Foundations of Prayer

In order to have a corporate attitude of prevailing prayer, it is first necessary for a body of believers to have solid foundations of prayer on a personal basis. Creating such solid foundations involves the posture and expectancy that come from meeting with the Lord in a place of intimacy and close fellowship. These foundations are required in order for God to address any issue of sin that must be dealt with and then to build His vision in and through us. Then, after giving us solid personal foundations, He can use us in a relationship of corporate prayer with others—who through personal prayer are also rediscovering identity, purpose, potential and vision in the Lord—to bring about revival and transformation. Without the foundation of prevailing prayer on a personal and then a corporate basis, the foundation for revival is weak and will not last long once the building commences and the enemy begins to launch his arsenal.

Our foundations *must* be in place before the building begins. Our first and foremost foundation must be in the

Lord through prayer, and beyond that we must create solid foundations with spouse, family and colleagues—the divine order as revealed in Ephesians. Unless we have relational unity acting as an adhesive for every foundation within the Church, it is difficult to identify what gaps have to be repaired and to see the project with the mind of the Lord. Furthermore, the absence of a solid foundation makes it difficult to identify and bind the enemy. The enemy always targets relationships, and often a building program can only go so far as the strength of our relationships and foundations permit. *This is one of the key reasons why revivals come to an end too soon.* When Satan causes disrepair or disorder, we must be able to repair that place so that the Lord can meet with His people once again, and it is essential for a solid foundation to be laid in order to be able to repair it when necessary. Thus, at all times, personal, prevailing prayer and transformation must precede corporate prayer and transformation. It is a clear, simple, indisputable principle!

What Is Prevailing Prayer?

As I have already indicated, the Church's preparation for revival is in many ways more important than the actual revival itself. Through proper preparation, God is able to position His people with a certain posture and authority that welcomes His presence into a community. While every Christian is called to pray, certain people have a special capacity to enter into a season of prayer and to do whatever is necessary to fulfill the vision and mandate God places on their hearts. Entering into prevailing prayer requires tenacity, aggressiveness and an unwillingness to yield to whatever pressure or challenge tries to divert attention from the task at hand.

Evan Roberts, whose name has become synonymous with the 1904–5 Welsh Revival, stated that it is a common mistake to become overly occupied with the *effects* of revival, rather than continuing to pray for and protect the original *cause* of the revival. That is, the effects of revival can become a distraction and deterrent if we lose our focus on the One who called us into that foundational place of intimacy. Roberts knew God would redeem the one hundred thousand souls for whom he had travailed in prayer, but he also knew that all the time he had to remain focused on the Lord who had entrusted him with this assignment. This focus is maintained through prevailing prayer.

The following quote by Kathie Walters in *Bright and Shining Revival* gives a clearer understanding of what prevailing prayer is, why it must take place before revival comes and why it must fervently continue once revival is here:

> Every revival that has broken upon the face of the earth has been preceded by men and women upon their knees travailing before God. Undeterred by cold and the discomforts of the barn; . . . undeterred by the fact that no one else seemed concerned about revival and the world was as godless as ever, they travailed and prayed. Kneeling in the straw or upon their faces in agony of soul, they cried before the throne. No half-hearted, sentimental, religious, half-doubting prayers to which the Church is so accustomed today, and which accomplish so little. These men wrestled with God, drawing into the spiritual conflict every power and energy they possessed.[5]

The men who had covenanted to stand for revival *prayed!* They stormed the throne room of God. God imparted to them a burning passion for the lost. Confidence in God gripped every word that fell from their lips. What depths of reaching out to God! They prayed until they travailed and travailed until they prevailed. They prayed until God answered. Travail must always precede "prevail."

Prayer That Gets God's Attention

The opening verses of Isaiah 64 refer to the presence of God coming upon His people and His nations. Verses two and three tell us that both nations and mountains tremble before His presence. Then the fourth verse offers these arresting words: "Since ancient times no one has heard, no ear has perceived, no eye has seen any God besides you, who acts on behalf of those who wait for him." It is God's desire to come into the midst of His people, and as this verse explains, God wants to act on behalf of those who wait for Him. But how do we get His attention?

In his book *The Price and Power of Revival,* Duncan Campbell refers to one of the prayers that clearly caught God's attention and served as one of the igniting sparks for the release of the Lewis Revival in the Hebrides.

"Lord, You made a promise—are You going to fulfill it? We believe that You are a covenant-keeping God, will You be true to Your covenant? You have said that You would pour water on the thirsty and floods upon the dry ground. I do not know how others stand in Your Presence, I do not know how the ministers stand, but if I know my own heart, I know where I stand, and I tell Thee now that I am thirsty, oh, I am thirsty for a manifestation of the Man of Thy right hand"—and then he said this—"Lord before I sit down, I want to tell You that Your honor is at stake."

Have you ever prayed like that? Here is a man praying the prayer of faith. . . . This is a man who believes God . . . who dares to stand solid on the promise of God and take from the throne what the throne has promised.[6]

Prevailing prayer attracts God's attention and allows Him to come and tarry in the midst of a people. However, coming into the presence of the Lord boldly can only happen with cleansed and expectant hearts—hearts that have addressed the horrific issue of sin and are prepared for the rendezvous with their almighty, sovereign God.

The Ingredients of Prevailing Prayer

If we could take an X ray of revival, we would see common ingredients of prayer that always attract God's attention. We already have seen that tenacity, aggressiveness, expectation and vision are essential ingredients of prevailing prayer. What other ingredients are essential?

In his book *Heritage of Revival* Colin Peckham refers to the praying people of Barvas who were instrumental in the revival in that community.[7] Peckham names four things that were governing principles in the prayer life of these people.

First, he makes reference to the fact that these people had a right relationship with God in their personal walks. Second, they maintained a conviction that God was a covenant-keeping God who would honor His engagements. They believed that if they met all the requirements, God would act on their behalf at the request of their prayers. Third, they realized that God must be given room to work in His own way and not according to their program: "God was sovereign and must act according to His sovereign purposes—but ever (keep) in mind that while God is sovereign in the affairs of men, His sovereignty does not relieve men of responsibility. God is the God of revival, but man is the human agent through whom revival is possible."[8] Finally, the people of Barvas prayed in expectation of a manifestation of God by which people would acknowledge that the sovereign God had come into their midst. In other words, a supernatural expectation framed the manner in which they prayed! Can it be any less for us today? Evan Roberts defined four simple steps for those who want to rekindle their passion for the Lord. He believed these steps would enable God's people to pray expecting His presence to come into their midst in the form of revival. Simply put, these steps included:

1. Confess all known sin.
2. Search out all secret and doubtful things.
3. Profess the Lord Jesus openly.
4. Pledge your word that you will fully obey the Spirit.[9]

Notice the importance of the posture and position of the people engaged in the actual prayer. No known issue of sin could be left unresolved, and a sense of expectancy and obedience in what God was calling His people to do on His behalf pervaded the prayer. Roberts also taught entire groups of people to pray with unusual expectancy. The words were simple, but the content was powerful. Note again the sense of expectation, the sense of tenacity and the sense of aggressiveness in believing that God would respond to these simple prayers from hearts and mouths that yearned for God's presence.

1. Send the Spirit now.
2. Send the Spirit powerfully now.
3. Send the Spirit more powerfully now.
4. Send the Spirit still more powerfully now for Jesus Christ's sake.[10]

This simple type of prevailing prayer proved its power as it began to release revival in other parts of the world. For example, as the Welsh Revival gained momentum it influenced missionaries in Korea, who began to expect a similar outpouring of God's presence *if* they prayed with the same degree of expectancy and tenacity. As Towns and Porter report in *The Ten Greatest Revivals Ever,* many of these Korean missionaries were motivated to intensify their prayers in order to experience in Korea what had been taking place in Wales.[11] Throughout 1907 and part of 1908, many missionaries met to pray and study the first epistle of John, which became their textbook for revival.[12]

Towns and Porter cite one example of what took place in January 1907 as a result of six months of prevailing prayer by the Korean Church, asking God for a mighty move of His Spirit. On this occasion fifteen hundred men came together to plead with God to move in their midst. One person said later, "We were bound in spirit and refused to let God go until He blessed us."[13] With all these people praying, there was still "a vast harmony of sound and spirit like the surf in an ocean of prayer."[14] Shortly afterward the entire building was filled with the presence of God. Such fervent praying contained all the ingredients of prevailing prayer and always attracts the attention of the living God! It is also, however, such fervent prayer that must be sustained and increased if we are to steward revival and the permeating power of God's presence in society into the next generation.

Praying with Desperation and Passion

In recent years I have had the privilege of meeting and working with a number of people directly involved in present-day revival. I am particularly blessed whenever I am with Ugandans! I remember one of their prayer leaders saying that the people of Uganda had to learn to pray with desperation and allow their comfort zone to be discomforted! On another occasion I heard the same leader say that they had started to pray with passion and asked

God to inconvenience their convenience! If we are going to pray in such a manner as this, we must expect certain consequences!

One of my favorite biblical examples of a person who modeled prayer that was birthed out of desperation and passion is Hannah. The first chapter of 1 Samuel tells of the life of Hannah and teaches us that *desperation* leads to *conception,* which in turn leads to *sacrifice* and then prepares the way for *transformation.* We are told in this chapter that Hannah and her husband, Elkanah, and his other wife, Peninnah, came from the tribe of Ephraim, which means "fruitful in the land of my suffering" (Genesis 41:52). Hannah was aware of her inheritance of fruitfulness, but she was not fruitful because she had no children. Her rival, Peninnah, who had children, reminded Hannah constantly of her barrenness. But Hannah remained a model of tenacity and prevailing prayer as she was provoked and irritated by her rival. She wept. She would not eat. She prayed in bitterness of soul (see 1 Samuel 1:10). She reminds us of Job: "Therefore I will not keep silent; I will speak out in the anguish of my spirit, I will complain in the bitterness of my soul" (Job 7:11). All this can be termed as *desperation.*

Hannah's example is a model for the Church. In many accounts of historical and contemporary revival, the people were fed up with life in its day-to-day monotony and spiritual barrenness. God has entrusted to the Church His authority and His commission to speak His word of salvation and destiny into the world. But very often, when we are faced with the complexity and perplexity of society, we all too readily give in and operate from the position of mediocrity. Hannah would have none of this!

In the person of Peninnah, we see that God often allows us to experience certain circumstances in order to provoke and irritate us into prevailing prayer! For example, so often in day-to-day life people become annoyed with the caliber and ethics of politics, education, the economy, health and welfare or even life in the church. These and other such everyday life experiences can be the very catalysts that God uses to provoke us into a place of fruitfulness. For Hannah, it was out of the land of suffering that desperation and then fruitfulness were birthed.

We can become desperate in our prayer lives in one of two ways. First of all we can face devastation. The events of September 11, 2001, released corporate trauma into many parts of the world. People were shocked by what they saw and heard, and their desperate prayers were borne out of that devastation. The second way to birth desperation in our prayer lives is to pray with passion. People of revival invariably have begun to see the barrenness of their land through the eyes of the Lord and to yell out to God for a visitation of His Holy Spirit. When God reveals to us the real state of our communities, cities and nations, we can be both devastated and filled with aggressive passion at one and the same time. For Hannah it *did* matter to her that she had no children. It *should* matter to us that our cities and nations are in the clutches of the enemy of God's people. It is our responsibility to relinquish our land from the influence of the enemy through desperate and passionate prayer, in order that we can enter into and inherit our destiny.

When people are desperate, they face their weaknesses and also their impossibilities. This is what happened to Hannah. It is also what happened in Wales, the Hebrides, Korea, Uganda, the eastern Arctic and wherever else God has met and continues to meet with His people in His reviving power. As Isaiah 62:6–7 reminds us, God invites us to give Him no rest on this matter until He establishes the fullness of His purposes in our midst. It was out of this desperation that Samuel was conceived!

Prevailing prayer requires a desperate willingness by the people of God to dislodge their personal comfort. It requires praying with such passion that our convenience is inconvenienced for His sake. If we are willing to have our comfort zones discomforted and our convenience inconvenienced, then we will experience a new release of passion. This passion will fuel aggressiveness and expectation in a way that we have never experienced before. When we come to this awareness, then we understand "the difference between *knowing* He is in the house and *encountering* Him in the house."[15]

Fueling Passionate Prayer

What does it mean to "fuel" prayer? I like the words of George Otis, Jr., who said, "Revelation is the paintbrush God uses to enliven the gray canvas of our everyday reality. Dabbed in the medium of information—details that sit on His palette like dollops of multi-hued paint—it yields to the Master's touch. With a few well-placed strokes, He liberates us from vagaries and boredom."[16] With these words of Otis's, we are challenged to view revelation and knowledge as required menu items for our diet of prayer. Revelation is understanding the facts at hand from God's perspective and the resultant knowledge is what motivates us to pray passionately.

Hannah was well aware of the facts at hand, which is why she entered into such a sense of aggressiveness and expectation before her son, Samuel, was even conceived in the womb! In other words, she was preparing her womb for a visitation.

Similarly, we can prepare the "wombs of our cities" and our nations when we begin to understand the facts at hand from God's perspective. Spiritual mapping, for instance, is a discipline of research that enables us to pray with greater insight and understanding—just as X rays enable a doctor to see the cause of someone's complaint that cannot be detected on the surface. In other words, on the surface we might see the results of affliction without understanding the cause of affliction. Understanding the causes gives us a greater burden—and the greater the burden, the more we will perceive what is taking place, and the more we perceive about the situation, the more we need to persevere and fight through the obstacles.

Let us look at another analogy. Without the necessary food that enables our bodies to keep functioning, we would soon become too weak and anemic to fulfill our day-to-day obligations. Similarly, a car needs fuel in order to function. In the same way, people of prayer need insight and information in order to satisfy their needs to keep on praying with perspective and insight. Otherwise, a sense of lethargy and apathy can develop, which leads to a loss of expectancy. This is a key reason for a revival ending long before God's purposes for that revival are fulfilled!

We must keep our prayer lives fueled because complacency and contentment are dangerous assaults upon prayer. We can all too subtly become like those earlier people of God who grew used to a regular diet of "manna and quail" and asked for a return to the cucumbers, melons, leeks, onions and garlic of Egypt: "But now we have lost our appetite; we never see anything but this manna!" (Numbers 11:6). Similarly, we can become blasé about having the presence of the Lord with us. Remember that part of Uzzah's sin was his over-familiarity with the Ark and his lack of intimate knowledge of the Lord.

The moment we sense "spiritual anesthesia" setting in, dulling our minds and hearts to such an extent that we prefer the old ways rather than having His intimate knowledge in our midst, then we must be careful! It is time for a fresh word from the Lord to fuel us in our prayers.

It is also time to pray with greater perseverance than ever before. Persevering prayer makes us willing to pay the price no matter what it takes, and we no longer question or analyze God's ability to answer while looking at our clocks. Instead, we set our goal toward the destiny and pray it into reality. It has been said that prevailing and persevering prayer is similar to climbing a mountain. It means engaging the extra gears that are found on four-wheel-drive vehicles. It means fasting, it means obtaining additional prayer support, and it may mean adding high praise and worship since the darkest hour is always before dawn. This is what prevailing prayer is all about. It means engaging prayer in the method of Isaiah 50:7: "Because the Sovereign LORD helps me, I will not be disgraced. Therefore have I set my face like flint, and I know I will not be put to shame."

On a final note, intercessors need to have regular updates on the effectiveness of their prayers and need to receive both correction and direction from the leadership at necessary times. When relationships are intact, this rarely causes problems, since the Lord Himself is at the foundation of the relationships.

Understanding destiny, receiving regular reports, being able to give feedback after times of passionate prayer and being partnered with other people of like mind who are willing to pay the price of prayer on their knees are all proven examples of the ways in which passionate prayer can be fueled and continually revitalized. When such partnership is engaged in by many congregations that constitute the Church in the city, an entire community can be set on the journey towards spiritual transformation. It is as if different pieces of the divine jigsaw puzzle suddenly come together to form a shape and design that gives insight and direction as well as excitement and purpose. In the end, when the barren womb is suddenly filled with anticipation of something that will soon give birth to God's destiny, the provocation and the irritation seem well worthwhile and expectant faith moves into operation: "Now faith is being sure of what we hope for and certain of what we do not see" (Hebrews 11:1). Expectant faith is the result of the people of God choosing to walk with the fear of the Lord in pulsating, prevailing prayer.

I was once told that it would be spiritually healthy for me to read Leonard Ravenhill's very challenging *Why Revival Tarries* at least once a year! The testimony of his prayer life minces no words:

> Surely revival delays because prayer decays . . . no man is greater than his prayer life. The pastor who is not praying is playing . . . the two prerequisites to successful Christian living are vision and passion, both of which are born in and maintained by prayer . . . few of us can remember the last time we missed our bed for a night of waiting upon God for a world-shaking revival.[17]

5

...

The Fear of the Lord

Beware of reasoning about God's Word—obey it.

Oswald Chambers

A call for persevering leaders and a call to prevailing prayer require that we understand what it is to live and minister in the fear of the Lord. This is another essential ingredient for stewarding the Lord's presence in our midst.

Listening with Eyes and Ears

On September 11, 2001, my wife and I were flying back home from a series of conferences in Australia. Our aircraft touched down briefly in Honolulu for refueling purposes, and then continued on towards Vancouver,

Canada. While we were en route to Vancouver, our captain informed us of the terrorism then taking place in the United States.

While we were not given all the details, we were given sufficient information about the horrific incidents. I leaned over to my wife and said, "Honey, life will never be the same again!" As I said those words, I felt the Holy Spirit suddenly speaking directly into my spirit. Among the words the Lord imparted to me were the following: *This is the end of the age of innocence. This is a wake-up call. You can never preach in the same way again—now there is a call for a new type of urgency. The spiritual plates of the world have shifted. Today the world is seeing on the physical realm what is really taking place in the spiritual realm, and My Church must respond accordingly. Listen to Me, and I will give you counsel in these searching days.*

These statements gave me a whole new perspective for the work of the Church in these early days of the twenty-first century. The world is involved in a major spiritual conflict, part of which is being lived out in our day-to-day lives.

Habakkuk was concerned over the apparent inactivity of the Lord during his day, when in the midst of perplexity and challenge, God responded with these very significant words: "Look at the nations and watch—and be utterly amazed. For I am going to do something in your days that you would not believe, even if you were told" (Habakkuk 1:5). By the beginning of chapter 3 Habakkuk could say, "Lord, I have heard of your fame; I stand in awe of your deeds, O Lord. Renew them in our day, in our time make them known; in wrath remember mercy" (Habakkuk 3:2). Before he got to the place where he could say these words, however, Habakkuk learned an invaluable lesson. Physically, Habakkuk stopped trying to get answers and started listening to God instead. Ponder these words in Habakkuk 2:1: "I will stand at my watch and station myself on the ramparts; I will look to see what he will say to me, and what answer I am to give to this complaint." Note that Habakkuk positioned himself on the ramparts in order to see and understand the reality of what was going on around him from God's perspective. He then said he would *look* and *listen* before he would respond.

One of the Scriptures God has impressed upon me in recent days is Psalm 25:14, "The LORD confides in those who fear him; he makes his covenant known to them." This is an amazing verse when we consider that the Lord actually wants to confide in the likes of you and me! In other words, He does not want to leave us ignorant of what is going on around us. He wants to share with us His intent and purpose as far as His involvement in our lives is concerned. But notice what He said two verses earlier: "Who, then, is the man that fears the LORD? He will instruct him in the way chosen for him." The person who fears the Lord is the one who is willing to be instructed by the Lord. How often do we really take time to listen to the Lord these days?

It is important to make a distinction between hearing and listening when it comes to our position with God. *Hearing* is the basic use of one of the five physical senses but does not necessarily include reception of what is being said. The *Concise Oxford Dictionary* in part defines the term as "to listen impartially" and "to be informed."[1] *Listening,* on the other hand, is the willingness to internalize what is being said and to assimilate the contents before giving a response. Again quoting the *Concise Oxford Dictionary,* to listen is "to make effort to hear something, (to) hear (a) person speaking with attention."[2] In Luke 8:18, Jesus says, "Therefore consider carefully how you listen. Whoever has will be given more; whoever does not have, even what he thinks he has will be taken from him." Jesus is saying it is important how we listen—otherwise, we might be working on the basis of presumption and assumption.

Unless we are listening to the counsel of the Lord it is very hard—if not impossible—for the Church to speak forth His prophetic words into the world with any sense of boldness and authority. I love these words of Jesus: "I tell you the truth, the Son can do nothing by himself; he can do only what he sees his Father doing, because whatever the Father does the Son also does. For the Father loves the Son and shows him all he does. Yes, to your amazement he will show him even greater things than these" (John 5:19–20). Jesus repeats these words in John 8:28: "I do nothing on my own but speak just what the Father has taught me." Jesus fully submitted Himself to the higher purposes of the Father. He listened and learned from Him before He said or did anything in the way of ministry.

In Matthew 10:19–20, Jesus counsels us not to worry about what to say or how to say it, even in the midst of adversity and challenge. He says that the Holy Spirit gives insight and instruction when our eyes and ears are open to Him. I believe that this is what happened when Samuel responded to the Lord saying, "Speak, for your servant is listening" (1 Samuel 3:10). Samuel learned what it was to listen to the Lord before he spoke forth the word of the Lord and later, in 1 Samuel 4, we read that Samuel's word went to all of Israel. Proverbs 1:7 refers to the fear of the Lord being the beginning of wisdom, but two verses earlier we read these words: "Let the wise listen and add to their learning, and let the discerning get guidance" (Proverbs 1:5). Even in the letters to the seven churches in Asia Minor given in Revelation 2 and 3, God exhorts His people to hear what the Holy Spirit is saying. I appreciate how the New Living Translation of the Bible explains the directive of Jesus: "Anyone who is willing to hear should listen to the Spirit and understand what the Spirit is saying to the churches" (Revelation 2:7 NLT). The implication is for us to keep on listening to the Holy Spirit. Listening to the Lord with our eyes and ears enables us to understand with greater clarity and insight the times in which we live, and then subsequently to speak forth His word in a prophetic way to a needy world.

The Key to Knowledge

Knowledge and obedience are both vital to understanding the fear of the Lord. In Luke 11:52 we read, "Woe to you experts in the law, because you have taken away the key to knowledge. You yourselves have not entered, and you have hindered those who were entering." These are serious words from the lips of Jesus Himself. When He refers to the key of knowledge He is, in fact, referring to the fear of God.

The fear of the Lord involves at least three key components. First, we need to be in awe of the Lord for who He is. Jesus Himself said that the greatest commandment is to "Love the Lord your God with all your heart and with all your soul and with all your mind" (Matthew 22:37). The writer of Ecclesiastes is wonderfully succinct in this matter: "Fear God and keep his commandments, for this is the whole duty of man" (Ecclesiastes 12:13). Malachi 2:5 puts it this way: "My covenant was with him, a covenant of life and peace, and I gave them to him; this called for reverence and he revered me and stood in awe of my name."

The second component is learning to be obedient to the Lord in spite of personal desires. Jonah, for example, did not particularly want to speak forth the word of God to Nineveh, since he did not believe the city deserved God's forgiveness or mercy. However, out of obedience to the Lord, Jonah eventually did what he was told. Understanding the fear of the Lord in our lives is learning to be obedient at all times, even if our opinion on the matter may differ from that of the Lord. He is, after all, the Alpha and Omega—He sees the beginning and the end all at once.

The third component of fearing the Lord is learning to hate evil with the same intensity as that of Jesus Himself.

This means rejecting whatever is wrong from God's perspective. David put it this way: "An oracle is within my heart concerning the sinfulness of the wicked: There is no fear of God before his eyes" (Psalm 36:1). David loved the Lord passionately and hated what the Lord hated.

The key to knowledge, then, is to fear the Lord. When we live and work in the fear of the Lord, we enter into a position of intimacy that allows us to listen to what the Lord wants to impart into our hearts. This is essential if we are going to be people who pray forth the reviving presence of the Lord, and then do what is necessary to sustain His presence in our midst. I love the words of Malachi 3:16: "Then those who feared the LORD talked with each other, *and the LORD listened and heard.* A scroll of remembrance was written in his presence concerning those who feared the LORD and honored his name" (emphasis mine). The Lord listened and heard those who understood the fear of the Lord in their lives and who talked and worked accordingly. To fear the Lord is to honor His name, and the Lord Himself responds accordingly.

Rest and Restoration

A close relationship exists between the words *rest* and *restoration.* The Lord calls us to come to Him, to take His yoke upon us, to learn from Him and subsequently to find rest for ourselves (see Matthew 11:27–30). This is intimately tied to the promise God gave Moses in Exodus 33:14: "My Presence will go with you, and I will give you rest." In no way at all does rest mean inactivity. If anything, it means entering into the full activity of God in and through our lives—but on His terms! In this regard, *rest* has a very close meaning to *restoration,* which is one of the synonyms for *revival* in Scripture.

Noah was obedient to the Lord in building the Ark, which served as place of refuge for all who chose to enter prior to the flood. The Ark was a testimony to God's faithfulness and His rest during the time the waters flooded the earth. The Ark, then, is a foreshadowing of something God wants to release upon and within the lives of His people.

Belief and Expectancy

However, so often our own testimony either inhibits or prohibits God from fulfilling His purposes in our midst. For example, Genesis 45 tells the story of Joseph being reconciled with his father and brothers. The news finally reaches Jacob that his son Joseph was alive: "Jacob was stunned; he did not believe them" (Genesis 45:26). Not until Jacob saw the carts sent by Joseph was he "revived" and "convinced" that his son was indeed alive (verse 27). This is an example of a person who has been traumatized into disbelieving even what God says is possible. In the end Jacob's spirit was revived and he was united with Joseph. It is interesting to note that so often we want God's refining fire in our midst, but due to a series of events and circumstances that took place perhaps years earlier, we are *traumatized* into an inability to receive anything from God.

It is so important to remove any negative mindsets and strongholds of thinking—whether in the life of the individual, the community or even the nation—that can subtly negate a move of God. The same issue is addressed in Malachi 3:13–14 when the Lord refers to His people who have said harsh things against Him: "You have said, 'It is futile to serve God. What did we gain by carrying out his requirements and going about like mourners before the Lord Almighty?'" (Malachi 3:14). The words and thoughts of the people themselves ensnared them into falsely believing that God would not act in their midst, or that nothing could be gained by preparing the way for His presence.

The same can be true today. God may want to restore an intimate relationship with His people, but it is as if His people are saying it simply is not worth it because God does not really mean what He says. Putting it another way, our minds and hearts are already predisposed and hardened against the probability of God's presence and activity in the lives of His people.

Revival simply will not happen until these false ways of thinking are addressed fully and honestly. Jesus Himself was confronted with this issue on many occasions. At times He could do few miracles in the midst of His people due to their lack of faith (see Matthew 13:58). On other occasions He rebuked them for their lack of faith and stubborn refusal to believe those who had seen Him following His resurrection (see Mark 16:14). The issues of belief and expectancy are critical in order to accept what God longs to do in the midst of His people.

One very alarming passage to ponder carefully is found in Hebrews 3:18–19: "And to whom did God swear that they would never enter his rest if not to those who disobeyed? So we see that they were not able to enter, because of their unbelief." One wonders how many times over the centuries the people of God—including us today—have missed out on His reviving presence due to an existing atmosphere of unbelief. Such a lack of faith is often upheld—wittingly or unwittingly—even in the Church itself. If revival is going to come to our communities and become authentic transformation that releases the presence and the glory of the Lord, the Church must maintain a high level of faith, expectancy and willingness to receive all God has for us. This must then be maintained and sustained since further mindsets and stronghold-thinking will undoubtedly challenge and confront us to the degree we choose to bring God's transforming power and presence into the very core of society. The deeper the impact, the higher the challenge!

Intimacy with God

Intimacy is an essential requirement for a move of God in our midst. At one level, intimacy with the Lord is all about personal transformation and being changed from one degree of glory to another (see 2 Corinthians 3:18). We need to experience personal transformation before we can pray with authority and authenticity for corporate transformation to take place. Putting it another way, it is very hard to pray for something that we ourselves have not experienced. There is, however, a deeper issue behind the whole subject of intimacy and revival.

David modeled an intimate relationship with God. Although not one reference in the Bible ever suggests that Saul loved the Lord, many references state quite categorically that David loved the Lord. David understood the root of intimacy with God. Psalm 51 gives significant insight into David's desire to worship God with all his being. In order to do so, he wanted to ensure that there were no transgressions in his life that would impede the grace, love and power of the Lord in and through him. David recognized that when he sinned, he sinned against the Lord (see Psalm 51:4). His desire was for the Lord to blot out all his iniquity (see Psalm 51:9), and for him to have a pure heart before the Lord in order that full praise could be given to the Lord (see Psalm 51:15–19). Similarly, when the people of God move into a deeper level of intimacy with Him, God can move them into a greater dependency upon Him.

History records that many revivals are lost when intimacy with God is compromised. Such compromise takes place because of disobedience and the subsequent loss of holiness in a people's relationship with God. So often revival tends to come to a peak and then leave because it cannot be maintained by the people who welcomed the Lord in the first place. In other words, the people stewarding God's presence do not have the capacity and endurance to *continue* to guard, keep and occupy His presence in their midst—an issue of stewardship we will examine in greater detail in chapter 7. Partly, this is due to a lack of intimacy.

Intimacy with God is essential to stewarding revival, and stewarding revival is essential if we are to ensure that the enemy does not steal the results of revival. It is not altogether uncommon for the leaders who prayed for revival in the first place to be the very ones in whom corruption, immorality, financial abuse and other such measures of sinful living are brought to the surface. We must focus on the Lord of the revival and not upon His catalysts of revival—otherwise, we may become shocked and in despair at what God reveals. God is clearly shaking all religious foundations and preparing us for a lasting revival built upon solid foundations of integrity, honesty, purity and accountability—in essence, intimacy with Him.

The end product of all revival is fruitfulness; this is due to the intimacy that God originally established as the essence of our relationship with Him. God commands His creation to be fruitful (see Genesis 1:22–28). Revival is a means by which we go back to any point of departure of this fruitfulness. In other words, revival returns us to the place of fruitfulness where God can work in and through the lives of His people. This requires our going back to an early beginning rather than relying upon a historical pattern.

Genesis 1:28 speaks of fruitfulness and multiplication, and this is also the type of fruit to which Jesus refers in John 15: "I am the vine; you are the branches. If a man remains in me and I in him, he will bear much fruit; apart from me you can do nothing" (John 15:5). In fact, Jesus is repeating the principle that the foundation or boundary stone for the fruit comes from His presence dwelling in our midst. Jesus also said it this way: "You did not choose me, but I chose you and appointed you to go and bear fruit—fruit that will last. Then the Father will give you whatever you ask in my name" (John 15:16). Jesus is always looking for ways to make us more fruitful, but as John 15:1 indicates, such increasing fruitfulness only comes as the branch abides in the vine—and this means intimacy with the Lord!

This principle, which is of such importance to the Lord, is found elsewhere in Scripture. Following the flood, for instance, He gave the same commandment and expectation to Noah: "As for you, be fruitful and increase in number; multiply on the earth and increase upon it" (Genesis 9:7). Every battle we face—whether spiritual, financial, relational or physical—is, in fact, an attempt to steal the intimacy between God and His people. When we engage in any sinful action—theft, sexual immorality, double-mindedness—we are actually engaging in the battle that is being fought over our intimacy with the Lord. Our sinful nature will try to substitute for the intimate cry that every human heart has for fulfillment. David understood this, which is why he was so adamant that nothing stand between him and the Lord. His entire being yearned for the Lord's presence.

As we have already discussed, when we have a deep understanding of the *fear of God* at work in our lives, then we also will have a working understanding of the *knowledge of God* at work in our lives. Paul considers this understanding to be part of our responsibility in ensuring that nothing interrupts *intimacy with the Lord* and His ongoing work in and through our lives: "We demolish arguments and every pretension that sets itself up against the knowledge of God, and we take captive every thought to make it obedient to Christ" (2 Corinthians 10:5). If the knowledge of God is stolen from us, then intimacy with Him is lost and we simply will not fear Him in the way that is required for us to pray as persevering leaders and as conscientious intercessors. Our authority, our position of stewardship upon the land—everything is based on the degree of intimacy that we have in our relationship with the Lord. Indeed, as John 15:16 says so clearly, we were appointed to bear fruit that will last.

Revival tends to wane after 24 to 36 months because *the stewards of that revival have not sufficiently positioned the fruit of the revival into the heart of society.* That is what this book is all about! In the beginning God created us to know Him, and it is this depth of intimacy that produces the lasting fruitfulness that God looks for in our lives. Ongoing intimacy and revival on the personal level enable us to keep on stewarding it at the corporate level. When an individual, a city or a nation reaches the depth of intimacy with the Lord that He intended from the very beginning— such as He had when He walked with Adam and Eve— then a pattern for lasting revival is established, and the Lord will indeed remain in our midst.

But, remember, we cannot base our understanding or expectation of revival upon an earlier historical move of God. Why? Simply because if the earlier revival came to an end, it was based upon something less than the original foundation that God required in His relationship with man. Any revival built upon any foundation other than that of intimacy with the Lord will eventually crumble. As Charles Finney and other such servants involved in revival have intimated, each of their revivals had unique weaknesses because the parameters of revival had never been clearly defined. If we base our understanding of revival on a person or upon history, or upon the expectation of supernatural manifestations of the Holy Spirit—or upon anything else other than what God intended to do when He walked with man in the Garden of Eden—then we are preparing *a false* foundation and will not experience lasting fruit. As Fish says, *"Experience-centered revivals are usually brief."*[3] Indeed, even if we want to have revival for the sake of revival, then we are displacing intimate knowledge of God for the experience of revival—which in the end can itself become an idol.

Less Activity—More Intimacy

It is at this point that many make a subtle error. We can be busily serving the Lord but be far away from Him. God wants us moving from the outer court of activity and sacrifice to the inner court of intimate ministry to the Lord. In his book *Rekindled Flame,* Steve Fry gives an honest testimony to a time God challenged him on this very issue: "You know that I love you and that I have called you and given you gifts and abilities. But like these priests, you have been serving Me in the presence of an idol. That idol is the god of vision and ministry. You have become so enamored with your ministry . . . that you have neglected intimacy with Me."[4] Fry goes on to say that ministry to God "means to cultivate intimacy with Him, to set aside devoted time for Him, to focus on Him and reflect on His beauty. To minister to the Lord is to worship Him."[5]

The God of Love asks for our love and adoration. God literally created us to experience Him. Paul says, "For in him we live and move and have our being" (Acts 17:28). When we understand this unique oneness we have in Christ—and He has with us (see 1 Corinthians 6:17)—the abuses and imbalances that often occur during a revival with no clear biblical foundation are removed. We need to know who we are in Christ and that our lives are "now hidden with Christ in God" (Colossians 3:3). Paul emphasizes this principle by quoting these words of God: "I will live with them and walk among them, and I will be their God, and they will be my people" (2 Corinthians 6:16). If we are to see the effect of the revival stewarded and extended correctly, then the Lord Himself must always be the focus of our attention and the passionate desire of our hearts.

Revival, therefore, should never replace Jesus as the passionate desire of our hearts. The goal is to know Jesus—not simply to have a revival. The mistake David made in bringing the Ark back to Jerusalem was that his method was based upon a historical pattern undertaken by the Philistines. Not until David researched what went wrong and sought the heart of God did he understand why Uzzah died. Simply put, he tried to position the presence of God on man's terms and sought a program rather than the presence of the Lord. God's desire was for intimacy with His people, since true revival comes from its leaders and intercessors who are walking in holiness and integrity. God was looking for—and waiting for—this intimacy, holiness and integrity before He would allow His presence to be brought into the city.

The same is true today. If revival is going to come to our communities and become authentic transformation that releases the presence and the glory of the Lord, then we must understand what it is to live and minister in the fear of the Lord. Therefore, knowing what it is to live and minister in the fear of the Lord involves an intimacy with God birthed in a high level of faith, expectancy and willingness to receive on God's terms all that He has for us. Only then can we effectively steward the Lord's presence in our midst.

Ecclesiastes 12:13 states this so succinctly: "Fear God and keep his commandments, for this is the whole duty of man." To fear the Lord is to minister to Him, to love, worship and honor Him, to hold Him in awe, to resist all forms of evil, and to be obedient no matter what the cost. Acts 13:2 states that this was the testimony of the early Church: "While they were worshipping the Lord and fasting, the Holy Spirit said. . . ." Just let that sink in for a moment. As we worship the Lord and seek His face, the Holy Spirit will speak to us!

God longs to live with us in this place of intimacy. David said it in such a profound way in these words from Psalm 63: "O God, you are my God, earnestly I seek you; my soul thirsts for you, my body longs for you, in a dry and weary land where there is no water. I have seen you in the sanctuary and beheld your power and your glory" (Psalm 63:1–2). What a destiny, to behold His power and glory in the sanctuary!

6

...

Sin, Dandelions and Polo Fields

The more God's people reckon with the devil in their praying, the more they will taste of the liberty of the Spirit in
dealing with the issues of life.

F. J. Perryman

God's warning regarding sin comes early on in Genesis:
"If you do not do what is right, sin is crouching at your
door; it desires to have you, but you must master it"
(Genesis 4:7). Isaiah speaks for many when he confesses
the issue of sin before the Lord: "For our offenses are
many in your sight, and our sins testify against us. Our
offenses are ever with us, and we acknowledge our iniq-
uities" (Isaiah 59:12).

When revival stirs up the people of God, sin tends to
come to the surface with extraordinary agility! When handled rightly, the sin is confessed and addressed immedi-

ately as a natural part of the revival. For example, one of the fruits of revival is salvation of the lost, when they suddenly recognize their sinfulness and accept the saving knowledge of Christ. After a season of time, however, if the people grow slack about the fear of the Lord, they tend to compromise over the issue of sin. History is replete with examples in which sin became a matter of compromise some time after revival started; it went unaddressed and this one issue alone has resulted in many revivals being short-circuited!

If authentic revival is going to bear the lasting fruit that God intends, then we—as persevering leaders, people of prevailing prayer and people who understand the fear of the Lord and who choose to walk in intimacy with Him— have a mandate to master sin when it comes crouching at our doors. Even in these early years of the twenty-first century, the Church at large faces growing controversy over such issues as the deity of Christ, salvation through the Person of Christ, the doctrine of atonement, the gender of God, the issue of same-sex marriage and the authority of Scripture, to name but a few. Standards are developing in the Church that will separate the sheep from the goats as far as the authority and authenticity of the Church of Jesus Christ is concerned.

These are harsh words, but we are living in a world of compromise. When it comes to the issue of sin, the Church cannot afford to take part if it is to be the authentic and prophetic voice of God in society today. Church leaders are called upon to guard the purity of doctrine and Scripture, but when we place Christianity on an equal footing with religions of the world and join fraternities and societies that compromise essential Christian teaching and practice, then we are accommodating apostasy. When we walk in the fear of the Lord, and do not compromise over the issue of sin, then we will be able to deal with sin when it beckons.

Let's look more closely at the effect of compromise on the Church and then tackle the adjacent issue of unaddressed sin.

Compromise: Oil and Water Do Not Mix

Two of the "in" words in the Church today are *relativism* and *justification*. I want to mention relativism in this discussion of sin because it is a slippery term that lends credence to issues that, in fact, are in blatant opposition to the Word of God. It opens the door wide to compromise.

According to Isaiah 24:5–6, defilement in the world is caused by the people—the stewards of the land—who have broken the everlasting covenant. The Church has said things in the name of the Lord that He Himself has never said (see Jeremiah 23:25–26). God does not mince words on the matter of change: "I the LORD do not change" (Malachi 3:6). God is not relative. He does not change according to the needs or issues of the day.

Recently, I was reading an article in *Charisma* magazine in which Justin Long outlined some of the major issues the Church needs to address.[1] For example, he stated that trusted church workers annually steal some $16 billion from church funds and that Christians spend more on annual audits ($810 million) than on all workers in the non-Christian world. Furthermore, he stated that 200 million children in the world are exploited for labor, and 35 million people are still slaves in this generation. He also stated that pedophile racketeers victimize some 5.8 million children, there are still 24 million practicing prostitutes in the world, and 250 million women are battered in their homes each year. Drugs? Each year approximately $47 billion worth of cocaine is sold in the world. This is not the time for compromise in the Church—this is the time for straightforward confession of sin and heartfelt lamenting over mankind's fallenness.

Why is this so important? Simply because the Church is called to be the prophetic voice of God in the world. That is, the Church must levy the authority and judgment of the Word of God upon society in order that righteousness and justice prevail, and sin and usury be removed. If we do not, society will attempt to neutralize the Church in her call as the authentic and authoritative sign of the Kingdom of God in the world today.

Even as I write these words, a litany of cases of sexual impropriety between clergy and children in a variety of denominations is being disclosed. Huge financial settlements are taking place, and we are still only scratching the surface of a sin that the Lord is undoubtedly uncovering. He desires that whatever is of Him remain in His Church, and whatever is not of Him must go. God has assigned this task to His Church! The spiritual principle has never been more apparent: We do reap what we sow. When leadership compromises the Word of God and defines it by the standard of the world, God help the Church!

There is no room for relativism in the Church. No revival has ever been—or ever will be—founded upon compromise. Furthermore, such compromise will almost certainly bring revival to an abrupt end since it is not possible to steward holy living while embracing unholy standards. God is a heart reader—not a lip reader!

Unaddressed Sin: Dandelions and a Polo Field

Some years ago I was driving with a friend in the country. It was almost harvest time, and we were admiring the many beautiful colors of the fields. We noticed one field clothed in a wonderful yellow, and initially we thought it might be a mustard seed crop. Upon closer examination, however, we saw that it was nothing more than a field of dandelions. These weeds tend to group together and endlessly assault gardens and lawns where their seeds fall. My friend commented on how beautiful the color was from a distance, but when one got closer to the scene, the dandelions were exposed for what they really were.

Such is the way of sin. It may appear harmless and even attractive from a distance. But upon closer inspection, sin can be exposed for what it really is and dealt with accordingly! If it is not, if it is allowed to go unaddressed, God's people will likely grow accustomed to it and simply accept it as part of a lovely landscape.

Here is another example.

A large field near where I live has captured my attention for many years. By and large it is little more than marshland. On one occasion it was purchased as a potential golf course. That project never came to pass, and it was next purchased as a possible polo field. For some years I watched hopeful polo players come to the field, only to leave in dismay because the ground was saturated with water. Several attempts were made to drain the field, but since the root of the problem—the low-lying ground and high water level—was never adequately addressed, the water always returned.

This polo field is also rather like sin. If we do not deal with the roots of sin, then its effects will always resurface—often at the time when God is calling us to undertake a specific initiative in His name. The devil always knows when best to use unconfessed sin to his advantage! When sin is crouching at the door and gains entry, the Church consequently loses its strength and becomes somewhat anemic in spiritual issues. Unaddressed sin can cripple the Church and prevent it from providing a pure and holy place for God's presence to dwell.

Giving a Foothold to the Enemy

In *Releasing Heaven on Earth* I looked in depth at the issue of sin upon the land. I explained Paul's reference in Ephesians 4:27 to the word "foothold" or "place"—which is based upon the Greek word *topos*. He was referring to the way in which sin is given an entry point upon the land through lack of stewardship by the people who inhabit it. Consequently, when sin is not addressed, the god of this world is given the right of access to that area (see 1 John 5:19). The word *world* is *cosmos* in the Greek, and it means "structures and systems; that which encompasses our day-to-day life and work."

In other words, the enemy—the god of this world—is given power in the spiritual realm to influence our thinking, working and living in physical areas where sin has not been removed. When sin is deeply embedded in an area, perhaps for generations, often a higher concentration of spiritual issues exists within that vicinity—perhaps more so than in an adjacent area. This is why people sometimes feel a higher concentration of spiritual heaviness in one area than in another.

In Ephesians 4:27, Paul warns the Church explicitly not to give any leverage or position of authority to sin. He makes this point in the context of relationships within the Body of Christ. His goal is for relational and functional unity to be maintained at all times. Unless we are living in a position of intimacy with the Lord, both individually and corporately, the attitude of our minds and the ways in which we relate with each other can develop into all forms of falsehood, anger and sin. As a result we give a "foothold" to the enemy and allow him into that particular situation—be it our lives, our churches, our businesses, our cities or our nations.

Sin has to be rooted out of the very foundation of our lives so that the original boundary God established can be restored—the boundary God set in the Garden of Eden for mankind to be in relationship with Him. As we have discussed, nothing less than intimacy with God produces lasting fruitfulness. This is a critical point if we want to understand how to steward revival and ensure that demonic activity does not return to any given area, whether on an individual or corporate basis.

Psalm 125:3 is also explicit as far as God's intention: "The scepter of the wicked will not remain over the land allotted to the righteous, for then the righteous might use their hands to do evil." God wants His land to be returned to the stewardship of His people so that they are not influenced by the evil intent that may have been either active or dormant on that land for many generations. In the spiritual realm, unaddressed sin in an area affects mindsets and strongholds and can at every level influence the people who live there. As the body of Christ, our stewardship responsibility is to ensure that the land is free of sin in order that it may yield its strength—this is the cry of the people in Psalm 85. God's people are asking Him to revive them again in order that the fullness of His purpose can be fulfilled, and that the intimacy they once had with Him can be restored. How can this be done? It is all a matter of understanding both dandelions and that soggy polo field!

Lessons Learned

Let's go back to the subject of dandelions. Some years ago our garden was full of them. It seemed that our garden was a receiving point for every single dandelion seed that floated around our neighborhood! We were on our hands and knees on a regular basis removing dandelions.

If ever we thought we had them all, the next morning they would be back again!

The removal of a dandelion requires the removal of the entire root structure. It is useless to snip it off even below ground level and think the problem is solved! That is the easy way of dealing with dandelions, but it is certainly not permanent. In the case of our garden, some of the original soil used for planting the grass was itself full of dandelion seeds, and so it was a matter of digging down to the original foundation and removing those annoying roots. This required full commitment from us, along with a visit from our local professional weed controller. We basically had to develop a new foundation for our grass! Today, a dandelion rarely ever appears in our garden—but we keep watch over it carefully. The moment an intruder even attempts to locate itself on our property, it is pulled out and dispatched to the nearest garbage can!

Do you see the parallel to the subject of sin in the Body of Christ? When a foothold of sin has been dislodged and removed, a church must remain vigilant over that important area of vulnerability. Even if the roots are removed, it seems that almost overnight another "dandelion" is in its place. Negative mindsets and strongholds are apt to return when the people cease being vigilant in the care and stewardship of their territory.

Now, what about that polo field? With a great deal of time and financial investment, the water problem was eventually fixed. Enormous ditches and trenches were dug, and once the necessary depth was reached, drainage could be undertaken successfully and a new foundation could be established. Bear in mind that this was done several feet under the surface of the grass, but what was taking place *under* the surface would in due course have a consequential effect *upon* the surface.

This is the same principle for preparing a community for revival! Persevering leadership, prevailing prayer, informed intercession, removing the sin impediments in the land and digging deep down into the spiritual foundations are all part of the necessary work of preparing the way for God's presence. All obstacles must be removed and spirits must be revived in order for mindsets to be changed. People are then able to expect—and believe for—a coming revival, a plentiful harvest and the Glory of the Lord residing in the midst of His people. Unless this takes place, the enemy of God's people will return and try to destroy the foundation. And unless we keep watch and are vigilant over the issues of compromise and sin, the demonic realm will have ongoing access to the areas over which God has given us responsibility.

"Spiritual agriculture" requires our participation with the Lord of the harvest in order to prepare for a harvest that will last. Jeremiah 1:10 puts it this way: "See, today I appoint you over nations and kingdoms to uproot and tear down, to destroy and overthrow, to build and to plant." This is why Jesus says in Matthew 3:8–10 that as His stewards we are to be about the business of producing fruit in keeping with repentance, but that the ax is already addressing those roots that impede this quality of fruit. Dandelions may look attractive from a distance, but they are in fact intrusive weeds that steal the rich soil from other plants. If roots are corrupt, then the fruit will be corrupt. The Church must not only recognize sin for what it is but address it without delay.

Jesus was uncompromising about addressing sin, dealing with it and telling the people to "sin no more." He then carried on with other Kingdom-of-God business. Jesus also said:

> Watch out for false prophets. They come to you in sheep's clothing, but inwardly they are ferocious wolves. By their fruit you will recognize them. Do people pick grapes from thornbushes, or figs from thistles? Likewise every good

tree bears good fruit, but a bad tree bears bad fruit. A good tree cannot bear bad fruit, and a bad tree cannot bear good fruit. Every tree that does not bear good fruit is cut down and thrown into the fire. Thus, by their fruit you will recognize them.

Matthew 7:15–20

Fish makes an interesting point with regard to public confession of sin: "Public confession brings healing to people who have been carrying around spiritual garbage . . . it results in tremendous spiritual healing. It encourages others to confess and forsake sins."[2] Fish's point is that people can be moved to make even public confession of sin during times of revival. However, it is important that these same people who have come under the conviction of sin also come to a full assurance of forgiveness. Otherwise, when people enter into what I term "spiritual stripteasing" and display their tainted garments in public, the emphasis shifts to the sin rather than to the glory of God, and revival can come to a very fast halt. Revival can be sustained, on the other hand, when the correct guidelines for confessing and dealing with sin are followed.

If we are to steward revival faithfully, then we must always be willing to deal with the issue of sin honestly and thoroughly. When the Body of Christ addresses sin and recurring sin in an honest way, then we enter into a new position of care and protection that God has entrusted to the Church. Conversely, history proves that when the Church reneges on this issue, sin in its variety of masks and disguises easily reenters the relationship between God and His people. Many church fellowships that have experienced revival have dwindled into spiritual receivership. The seeds of revival need to be cared for and protected and nurtured, even after the harvest has begun. This is a critical spiritual principle to understand if we want to maintain the presence of the Lord in our midst.

However, this principle leads us to another searching question: If we are dealing with the subject of revival that recedes, is it possible to "re-seed" revival? Since we are called to steward the territory, let's continue on this journey and find an answer to that question.

7

...

Stewarding the Territory

While its promoters keep humble, and in a prayerful spirit while they do not retaliate but possess their souls in patience, while they do not suffer themselves to be diverted, to recriminate and grieve away the spirit of prayer, the work will go forward.

Charles Finney

So far we have addressed a number of reasons why revival leaves after a season. We have reviewed some of the various measures God entrusts to His Church to ensure that when His presence is stewarded correctly, there is a much greater likelihood that His power and glory will descend upon society. We have looked at the importance of persevering leadership, prevailing prayer, what it means to live in the fear of the Lord and maintain intimacy in relationship with Him, and the importance of not compromising over the issue of sin. God also calls us to steward the territory—that is, to take on a responsibility of guardianship over the land He entrusts to His people. It is in this area of responsibility that revival often begins to recede, leaving many unanswered questions.

Boundaries and Foundations

In order to provide some answers to these questions, we need to study some critical boundaries and foundations of revival and our relationship with God. Ecclesiastes 9:18 says, "Wisdom is better than weapons of war, but one sinner destroys much good." In the context of this passage a sinner refers to somebody who has removed certain God-given boundaries that ensure a fruitful life. Consequently, his life destroys much potential fruitfulness. Boundaries are critical because they provide a means of protecting the fruit God wants us to produce.

In biblical days a landlord would position a watchtower in his vineyard and surround the vineyard with a wall. The wall and the watchtower gave the vineyard necessary protection to assure its growth and fruitfulness (see Matthew 21:33). Without these boundaries, the land would be left vulnerable.

The vineyard represents the fertile soil of our hearts. It is intended to produce a wine void of any inhibition in expressing our love for Him. It is that part of us that produces an intimate, heartfelt response to the Lord. In Isaiah 5:1–7 we read of the vineyard the Lord established for us in which the stones were cleared away and the choicest of vines planted. However, it yielded only bad fruit because, as the passage indicates, sin was allowed to enter. As a result, the wall was removed and the people suffered the consequences. God removes His protective presence from our midst when sin enters into the vineyards of our hearts. When no boundaries or parameters are in place to protect what we are trying to establish in the name of the Lord, then we have no biblical foundation for revival, and we easily destroy much fruit.

When these boundaries and foundations are removed, we enter into the state of lawlessness referred to in 2 Thessalonians 2:7. One contemporary example of such lawlessness is humanism, which always tries to remove biblical boundaries that help us to discern between what is godly and what is sinful. Proverbs 22:28 addresses this issue directly; we are told not to overlook an ancient boundary stone established by our forefathers. Similar instruction is found in Proverbs 23:10, where once again we are told not to move an ancient boundary stone or to encroach on the fields of the fatherless. The New Living Bible translation of Proverbs 23:10 is quite explicit: "Don't steal the land of defenseless orphans by moving the ancient boundary markers, for their Redeemer is strong. He himself will bring their charges against you." Deuteronomy 19:14 gives even further instruction on this important issue: "Do not move your neighbor's boundary stone set up by your predecessors in the inheritance you receive in the land the LORD your God is giving you to possess." When boundary stones are established by the Lord and then removed, God's people are vulnerable to all types of lawlessness and sin—including usury, jealousy, lust, theft, presumption and pride.

If we are willing to work within the boundaries and principles the Lord gives for revival, then we can equip ongoing generations to maintain the presence of God at every level of society. Otherwise, revival will be temporary, lasting only a few years and affecting only a small percentage of the population, and the next generation of leadership must begin the process of establishing boundaries and foundations all over again.

As we saw in chapter 2, God's people often mistakenly return to the last event identified as revival, rather than to what God wants us to identify and experience: the power of His presence. This is what lay behind David's attempt to transfer the Ark back to Jerusalem. No proper plans were made, nor did the people have any understanding of God-given boundaries. They resorted to the way the Philistines had transferred the Ark, and when Uzzah tried to reposition the presence of God in his own way, he died and the attempted revival immediately came to a screeching halt.

The Church of the twenty-first century needs to understand that many modern-day Uzzahs are perishing in the name of revival simply because they are misusing, misrepresenting and misunderstanding how to handle the holiness of God. Like David, we do not understand the correct parameters for welcoming the presence of the Lord, and we have not put sufficient boundaries in place. At times we try to steal other people's boundary markers or try to build on someone else's foundations without realizing that they themselves were built on man-made programs and not on the presence of the Lord. Thus, researching why revivals come to an end is vital because we can learn how to sustain the presence of the Lord. When we understand what a model of revival is all about and then exemplify it, parameters can be established properly and the fruit of revival can be protected. Only in seeking answers can we have His security established around us and allow Him to be a watchtower in our lives.

A Biblical Model for Revival

Does Scripture provide any boundaries for revival? Mark 12:27 says, "[God] is not the God of the dead, but of the living." Several times in Scripture we find Jesus say-ing that God is the God of the living. He is the God of life. Revelation 1:8 says Jesus is the Alpha and the Omega— the beginning and the end—and He is both at the same time. In His own words He is the One who is, who was and who is to come (see Revelation 1:4, 8). This is impor-tant in understanding that the God of life is also the God of revival. Scripture contains approximately fifty different words in Hebrew or Greek that refer to the word *life,* and in many places such words refer to life that has been renewed or restored. Therefore, our model for revival comes from God, and Jesus illustrates this model in His own birth, death and resurrection.

God wants us to experience His abundant life. Conse-quently, the doctrine of resurrection is foundational to revival. And if Jesus is our model for revival, then He also gives us the parameters for revival. The principles of revival, therefore, cannot really be put into action until we understand the doctrine of resurrection. In chapter 1 we looked at several definitions for the term *revival.* Each refers specifically to making something alive again that was dead. Psalm 23:3 reads, "He restores my soul." This word *restore* is the same word used many times for the word *revive,* and it means to take something back to the point of departure.

One of the closest biblical words for *revive* or *revival* comes from the Hebrew word *chayah (khaw-yaw),* which primarily means to live or make alive, nourish up, pre-serve alive, quicken, recover, repair, restore or be made whole.[1] Interestingly, the first four times this word is trans-lated as "revive" in the Authorized Version, it deals with four increasing levels of death:

1. Genesis 45:27, a Scripture we examined earlier, depicts Jacob as an old man with a lost dream. How-

ever his spirit is *revived* when he sees the wagons Joseph had sent to carry him.
2. In Judges 15:19, Samson is close to death due to lack of water. God "open[s] up the hollow place in Lehi, and water [comes] out of it." When Samson drinks, his strength returns, and he is *revived*.
3. In 1 Kings 17:21–22, Elijah restores a woman's newly dead child. Elijah calls out to the Lord, and the Lord hears Elijah's call. The boy's life returns; he is *revived*.
4. Finally, 2 Kings 13:21 tells the extraordinary account of a dead man being thrown into the grave of Elisha. Upon touching Elisha's bones, the dead man suddenly is *revived*, and he stands up on his feet.

It is important, therefore, to understand that death is required before revival can occur. Jesus was born, He lived and died, and He was resurrected; therefore, He demonstrated that revival is possible! He Himself says, "I am the resurrection" (John 11:25). When we recognize His sacrifice and the power of His resurrection, we put to death what went wrong before and put back into place whatever has to be made right in our relationship with God. Whatever keeps us from experiencing the intimate love of God must, subsequently, be put to death in order for our intimacy with Him to be resurrected—and restored. Thus, the resurrection of Jesus allows the intimacy that Adam and Eve had with God in the Garden to be restored in and through us. His death had to come before revival could occur for us.

Revival is not for the lost, nor is it for the unsaved; revival is for the Church. It is returning the people of God to that place of departure where they ceased experiencing the life of fruitfulness that God intended in the promise of Genesis 1:28. We are returning to that point of departure, and then being resurrected in that intimate life-giving relationship.

Throughout the Old Testament, life is determined by faithfulness to the righteous and holy standards of the Word of God. In the simplest sense possible, then, revival is a heartfelt return to a life of faith and the living and written Word, having put to death whatever has separated a person from God's intimacy and life-giving spirit. As Charles Finney once said, "Revival is nothing other than a new beginning of obedience to God."[2]

So our primary biblical model for revival is the resurrection of Jesus. But a second significant model lies in the account of David's attempt to bring the Ark back to Jerusalem: the model of death. David's intent was heartfelt and righteous: "O God, you are my God, earnestly I seek you; my soul thirsts for you, my body longs for you, in a dry and weary land where there is no water. I have seen you in the sanctuary and beheld your power and your glory" (Psalm 63:1–2). He had experienced the intimacy of God in the sanctuary, and now his whole being longed to see this relationship restored with Jerusalem.

But when David initially tried to return the Ark to Jerusalem, a boundary was broken. The procession began with no preparation and no organization, and the Ark was carried on the cart pulled by oxen. It is important to understand why the oxen stumbled at the threshing floor (see 1 Chronicles 13:9). In those days a six-pronged fork was used to remove the husks from the grain on the threshing floor. In Scripture, six is the biblical number for man, and in Old Testament days the pronged fork was a symbol of man working the land. Taking the analogy further, the scriptural threshing floor, then, as alluded to earlier, represents the meeting place between God and man. In this particular situation the oxen symbolize leadership, as they do in 1 Timothy 5:18, where Paul refers to leadership as oxen. The oxen—representing the leadership—stumbled because David and his people had not sought God's plan, and as a result a boundary was broken.

Death had to take place in order to remove the man-made way of trying to restore intimacy with God. 2 Samuel 6:13 says, "When those who were carrying the ark of the LORD had taken six steps, he sacrificed a bull and a fattened calf." Note that this particular sacrifice took place every six steps all the way into Jerusalem—about ten miles! Each time the procession stopped to sacrifice, fourteen animals were laid on the altar (cf. 1 Chron. 15:26)! Again, six steps represent man, and since seven is the biblical number of the Lord, fourteen represents giving a double portion unto the Lord. Somewhere between six hundred to four thousand people were part of this procession and were, therefore, walking through a very bloody pathway! This was the magnitude of the sacrifice that was required to atone for the sin of the people before the presence of the Lord could be restored in their midst. Once this process was complete, everything was in order: The Ark was restored to its rightful place, along with the worship and praise, the offerings and gifts. Indeed, restoration comes at all levels when the presence of the Lord is established in the midst of His people. It is clear to see from this account just how serious an issue this is to the Lord.

A third biblical model for revival, along with resurrection and death, is found in the life of Job: restoration. Job 42:2 states, "I know that you can do all things; no plan of yours can be thwarted." After experiencing death in many ways, Job found how to get back to the point of departure and into that place of restoration with the Lord. Job prayed for his friends (see verse 10), and then the Lord was able to restore his losses. When we pray for those who have brought grief into our lives or our cities or our nations, and we choose to put to death whatever has caused a breach in our relationship with God, then we are back to that original place of departure. We are then able to begin to move forward into revival, and our losses begin to be returned sevenfold.

These three biblical models teach that revival opens the door for a harvest of fruit that will remain for many years, so long as it is stewarded properly. Revival reconciles us to God and takes us back to an intimate relationship with Him. I like what Pablo Deiros says in *The Rising Revival*:

> In my opinion, a spiritual revival is neither restructuring, nor renewal, nor updating, nor restoration, nor revitalization, nor reformation, although all of these may come about as a result of revival. The essence of spiritual revival is a combination of dynamic ingredients which moves the Church to return to its theological roots in the Scriptures, accompanied by a missionary commitment in obedience to the lordship of Christ and under the power of the Holy Spirit. The Church was constituted by Jesus Christ to fulfill a mission. Consequently, spiritual revival has to do basically with the recovery with the reason for being (raison d'être) of the Church. . . . Every time the Church surrenders itself in obedience to the Lordship of Christ and is filled with the Holy Spirit, committing itself to the mission of God in the world, the supernatural manifestation of God's voice that we call "revival" occurs.

> An authentic spiritual revival is the result of a deep outpouring of the Holy Spirit in the lives of those who have been regenerated by Him according to their faith in Christ as Lord. . . . This results in the outreach of the Church to the world to proclaim the gospel of the Kingdom. . . . An authentic spiritual revival always coincides with evidence of the powerful action of God, through His people who have become spiritually renewed and obedient, for evangelization.[3]

The Church as Steward of the Land

God has given man the responsibility of looking after what belongs to Him; the definition of *steward* is simply

"one who is looking after the property of somebody else."
So in maintaining revival, what else does God want us to
steward?

God gives man responsibility for the land he inhabits,
and land is the original meeting place between God and
man, as referred to in the Torah. "The land must not be
sold permanently, because the land is mine and you are
but aliens and my tenants. Throughout the country that
you hold as a possession, you must provide for the redemp-
tion of the land" (Leviticus 25:23–24). As the steward of
the land, the Church has the responsibility to remove from
the land whatever brings dishonor to the Lord. Sixty-five
percent of Jesus' teaching is parabolic, and of that approximately 35 percent deals with the issue of stewardship and
the responsibility of God's people to recover for our Lord
what has been lost, hidden or destroyed.

As I mentioned in *Releasing Heaven on Earth*, when we
are faithful stewards to what is entrusted into our care,
the land yields its strength and reflects the higher purposes
God has for His people who dwell and work in that area.
Conversely, if the people are not worthy in their stewardship responsibility, then the land reflects such fallen
stewardship. I referred specifically to the four major clas-
sifications of fallen stewardship, also called sin and defilement: idolatry, immorality/fornication, bloodshed and broken covenants. I explained why God has to judge such
conditions, and why as a result we experience famine, ecological devastation, war and disease.

In his book *Sowing Seeds for Revival*, Martin Scott defines
a fifth classification.[4] He believes this is a pressing issue in
every generation and can become another means by which
the land is healed. Scott is referring to intergenerational
relationships such as Scripture describes: "He will turn the
hearts of the fathers to their children, and the hearts of
the children to their fathers; or else I will come and strike
the land with a curse" (Malachi 4:6). "'Honor your father

and mother,' which is the first commandment with a promise—that it may go well with you and that you may enjoy long life on the earth" (Ephesians 6:2–3).

When restoring intergenerational relationships, the people are utilizing their God-given authority to remove from the land what does not bring Him honor and glory. When generations are restored in their relationships with each other and the parents prepare to release the children for their new "wineskin" of ministry, then God's blessings bring fruitfulness to the land.[5] The curse on the land is removed, and the land prepares for a new season of harvest. Here is what Scott says in this regard:

A colleague of mine, Stuart Lindsell, pointed out to me the potency of John 10:40–42 when understood against the backdrop of the issues surrounding land. We read,

Then Jesus went back across the Jordan to the place where John had been baptizing in the early days. Here he stayed and many people came to him. They said, "Though John never performed a miraculous sign, all that John said about this man was true." And in that place many believed in Jesus.

The immediate chapters have born testimony to the unbelief of many Jews, particularly in the Jerusalem context. However, this passage is full of geographical references, and if ever there was a locality in the gospels that had been the recipient of humble repentance, surely this was one of the key places. In that place the ground was fruitful, it began to yield up a harvest of salvation as "many believed in him there" (nrsv). Land can be healed; it can become fruitful, but only as repentance takes place.[6]

This is another return to a point of departure that affects the people who live on the land, the people in their relationship with God and the land in its relationship with God. This is why I refer to the Church as the *steward of the land.* Through proper stewardship, the Church opens up the land to receive the full blessings and destiny that God has prepared for the people who live and work there. As the prophetic voice of God, the Church is given the key to open the door and allow the Lord entry into that place.

In *Releasing Heaven on Earth,* I also mention the blessings of God as listed in Leviticus 26. These blessings are distinguishing marks upon the land that normally accompany the transforming power of God. They are: ecological health, economic health, personal security, civil security, international security, honor and growth, and innovation and creativity.[7] These blessings upon the land are evidence of the promise of fruitfulness that God gave to Adam and Eve in Genesis 1:28. They also testify to the promise He gives His people in John 15: the promise of abiding fruit that comes from an intimate and lasting relationship through Christ.

When to Re-Seed and Not Recede

In the course of my traveling over the last several years, I have visited a number of areas where revival has taken place historically. I have almost always noted the same common denominators, or components, involved in the initial release of revival, these being persevering leadership, prevailing prayer, a fear of the Lord, a willingness to enter into ongoing repentance and travail, and a willingness to deal with whatever issues of sin may have existed upon the land. Putting it another way, there was something in these components that caught God's attention. Even if only for a short season, He tarried with His people in these places. The question is, when this has happened once in a certain location, can it happen there again?

Many different nations in the world have experienced stirrings of revival on a number of occasions. For example, in 1923, Charles Price visited Victoria, Canada, and a large percentage of Victoria's population at that time became actively involved with the church. Not only did church attendance grow, but also supernatural manifestations such as physical healing took place on an ever-increasing basis. This became a concern to local medical personnel, and at the same time pastors and church leaders began to fall prey to the fear of man. The pastoral leaders who had issued the invitation to Price suddenly withdrew their support of him. As a result, Charles Price was incarcerated, the revival stopped and Price soon left the city. Clearly, an offense took place in the spiritual realm. Can revival be re-seeded in a place such as Victoria?

The answer is *yes!* If God originally visited a place such as this with His glorious presence and certain attractors for His presence were in place at the time, it can definitely happen again. It is more a matter of dusting off the welcome mat and removing whatever weeds have covered the pathway of welcome since that time. This involves recognizing what went wrong in an earlier attempt to welcome God's presence into a community, a process that becomes a precious teaching tool in enabling us to plan for the future.

But as we start this process, we are merely picking off dandelion heads unless we get to the root of the issue. We must find out what needs to be addressed in order for the glory of God to be released in that area. If the enemy has particular interest in keeping an area under his bondage and control, we need to ask why this is the case. In *Sowing Seeds for Revival*, Scott makes reference to the way in which the people of God and occult powers at times contend for the same "wells." He says:

> In our prayer journeys I have noted that there seems to be a focus by occult powers on some ancient territories, to

such an extent that they seem to wish to contest with us over the same "wells" as we do (Genesis 26:17–33). Some of the early sites that broke through to 24-hour continual prayer today are sites that are full of occultic presence.[8]

Genesis 26:12–15 describes how the wells of Isaac, which had been dug by the servants of His father, Abraham, were filled up and destroyed by the Philistines because they were envious and jealous of Isaac's wealth and prosperity. Isaac reopened those wells and developed new wells, which signified the extension of territory that God was giving to him.

Similarly, we must be stewards of the "wells" in our communities that were built and entrusted to us by our heavenly Father. Each community, city and nation in the world has its own particular distinctness, and if the well of life is not flowing in a way that brings God honor and glory, then we need to undertake whatever measure is necessary to re-dig the well. Doing so involves recognizing what God placed there in the beginning that was distinct and unique to that area but that became an issue exploited by the enemy. Scott also alludes to this in his book.[9] If we are going to undertake some necessary re-seeding, or re-digging of ancient wells, and understand that the presence of God has come and gone in certain areas, then we need to be about the business of digging up "the old anointings to see them restored for the Body of Christ. Let the old anointings keep calling, all the way back to the Upper Room."[10]

Such as with any territory, be it a garden or a nation, re-seeding requires careful attention. We are given the responsibility to undertake whatever it is that needs to be uprooted and removed: "See, today I appoint you over nations and kingdoms to uproot and tear down, to destroy and overthrow, to build and to plant" (Jeremiah 1:10).

Revival that has receded can be re-seeded. The wells can be re-dug. Once we learn what was involved in the past offense, we can rectify it today in both the spiritual and physical realms, so that the glory of the Lord may return and visit His people. Because of this responsibility of stewardship, the Church is seen as the guardian of the land.

The Church: Guardian of the Land

We have reviewed a number of principles that constitute the foundations and boundaries required for sustaining authentic revival. However, if revival and the resulting fruit are to last more than just a few years, then the Church needs to learn *how* to guard and embrace what has been entrusted into its care.

Guard, Keep and Occupy

Matthew 12:43–45 paints a clear picture of what happens when a house is not guarded or protected:

"When an evil spirit comes out of a man, it goes through arid places seeking rest and does not find it. Then it says, 'I will return to the house I left.' When it arrives, it finds the house unoccupied, swept clean and put in order. Then it goes and takes with it seven other spirits more wicked than itself, and they go in and live there. And the final condition of that man is worse than the first. That is how it will be with this wicked generation."

Luke 11:24–26 gives a similar account:

"When an evil spirit comes out of a person, it goes through arid places seeking rest and does not find it. Then it says,

'I will return to the house I left.' When it arrives, it finds the house swept clean and put in order. Then it goes and takes seven other spirits more wicked than itself, and they go in and live there. And the final condition of that man is worse than the first."

These passages certainly challenge our Western worldview. If we do not believe in the existence of evil spirits, then we have a problem at the outset. And even if we do accept that evil spirits exist and can affect people, we may have a hard time believing that these evil spirits want to inhabit cities and nations. Scripture holds sufficient evidence to support this viewpoint, and countless books have been written on the subject.

To me, it is clear that people, cities and land all are represented in this passage. All require the removal of evil spirits and the establishment of godly occupancy. We are called to guard, keep and occupy the land entrusted to us. We must remove the "wild animals" from the land and pray for God's healing and destiny upon His people, His cities and His nations. Thus, the result of revival in the Church should be a healthy harvest throughout society.

But it does not end there. If we are to be faithful stewards, we have to continue to keep watch over that which God entrusts to us. If our attention is diverted, the enemy can appear as a wolf in sheep's clothing and reestablish an earlier foothold, subtly embracing people with compromise. Before we know it, the land is once again under siege. Just as we disciple people in their growth in Christ, so we must keep watch over what is taking place around us. As the purposes of Christ continue to unfold in any given area, other levels of demonic infestation also will have to be addressed. Therefore, ongoing deliverance will most likely take place upon that land until the reflection of the Lord comes forth in every part of the city and the nation.

I have worked with churches that began the initial ministry of healing and deliverance within their communities and upon their land. We more or less felt the work was done! But within a year all forms of trouble returned, some much worse than before. It devastated eldership, ravaged intercessors, resulted in financial loss for the church, and led to despair and discouragement for the leadership involved. We need to remember what Gerald Fry learned regarding guardianship during the time of revival in his church. Fry recognized that certain issues eroded and weakened the work God had been developing in their midst. The revival was not being stewarded, and compromise resulted—even in areas of worship and prayer.

Malachi 2:16 says, "So guard yourself in your spirit, and do not break faith." Similarly, Philippians 4:7 says, "And the peace of God, which transcends all understanding, will guard your hearts and your minds in Christ Jesus." The word *guard* comes from a root word *phroureo* meaning "to garrison your hearts" or "to form a protection of militancy around that which is of high significance to the individual and to the Lord; to be a watcher and a sentinel; to post spies at the gates!"[11] Earlier we looked at the importance of the vineyard being surrounded by a wall and protected by a watchtower (see Matthew 21:33; Isaiah 5:1-2). This is what guarding, keeping and occupying is all about! It means that the Church forms a prayerful network of militancy both around and within that which God has called us to occupy and to care for on His behalf. As we undertake this on a regular basis, we ensure that God's destiny for us, our cities and our nations will continue to emerge, and that we will not lapse into the earlier lifestyle that was under siege with negative bondage and mindsets.

We must never forget that sin is crouching at the door, and that it desires to have us (see Genesis 4:7). Our mandate is to master sin before it tries to overcome us. The watchtower is one of the many biblical synonyms for the word *stronghold*. Our intention must be to ensure that the Lord is our stronghold in all that we undertake in His name (Psalm 27:1).

Nurture New Territory

Let's return briefly to the description of the polo field. Earlier this year our area experienced large amounts of rainfall. Previously, the polo field would have become something of a lake that attracted all the ducks from surrounding areas! This time, the adjacent land was fully submerged, but the polo field was clear! With the exception of one solitary little puddle, the drainage system worked perfectly. But in addition to the good drainage project, something else protected the polo field: The people who now have responsibility for looking after the field were watching over it carefully. In other words, they were guarding, protecting and nurturing their territory! If at any moment they saw a problem appear, they addressed it immediately.

As God's stewards, we too must nurture any new territory that experiences His reviving presence. We must keep watch over the territory that God assigns to the church in that particular area. If anything takes place—whether in the political, economic, educational or recreational realms— that may be in contradiction to the purposes of the Lord, then the church must begin to address the problem immediately! At no time must the enemy be given any access whatsoever to our life, work, relationships or ministry, thus preventing him from establishing a new foothold or from regaining a foothold that he had at an earlier time. We must be vigilant so that when the Lord sees something that is taking place He can prompt us to act.

Nurturing territory also means looking after leadership relationships. When it comes to the issue of revival, every leader who sticks out his or her neck in the name of the Lord will almost inevitably go through a fiery furnace experience due to the many issues that are being addressed in both the spiritual and physical realms. It is so important that the leadership does not tire out or wear out. E. C. W. Boulton wrote the following concerning the leadership of George Jeffreys:

> Each new advance brought its additional burden of oversight. The new position captured must be consolidated; the new converts made must be shepherded; the believers brought into fresh blessing must be fed. And all the time the work was gathering responsibility, God was graciously pouring out that sufficiency of strength which made those youthful workers equal to the tasks imposed upon them.[12]

As Boulton also points out, a leader needs to be able to inspire his followers with a spirit of unquenchable and incomparable zeal.[13] But leaders must not have between them any sense of jealousy or competitiveness, and they must be able to pass the baton when necessary. The leadership team must recognize who can take up the reins and who needs a brief sabbatical. All are going in the same direction, and no one is in competition with anyone else. This is important because the leadership relationships must be nurtured in order to stay strong and intact, and it is also the reason why others must stand in the gap and pray for those called to leadership.

During the years of "March for Jesus," I served as chaplain to the national board of "March for Jesus" in Canada and worked with other leaders throughout the world. I began to notice that one of the most common mistakes of that movement took place on the day after the actual march, which was often the most vulnerable day for leadership. After several months of intensive work, ministry, prayer and meetings the event came to a climax on the day of the march. The next day, the people were tired and wanted a break. They usually decided not to meet again for a few months, when preparations for the next march would begin. However, it was at this moment that leadership was at its most vulnerable, when the enemy looked to see if the territory of leadership remained "unoccupied." Months later, when we tried to convene leadership meetings, jealousy, apathy, indifference, individualism and aloofness—indeed, all the opposites of John 17 and Psalm 133—would invariably be evident.

If we are serious about revival, then we must be willing to do whatever is required to sustain the leadership, for they will be called upon to ensure that the revival is protected. This also requires our willingness to pray corporately for all the inter-church venues—the ministries, the all-night prayer meetings, the times of fasting and the overall decision making—that must be undertaken by the "city church" (meaning unified local church fellowships) to protect the territory under its care. All of this is crucial to nurturing the new territory.

Nurture Expansion

Isaiah 54:2 reads, "Enlarge the place of your tent, stretch your tent curtains wide, do not hold back; lengthen your cords, strengthen your stakes." And verse 3 says, "For you will spread out to the right and to the left; your descendants will dispossess nations and settle in their desolate cities." These important verses offer insight into the work of expansion that is part of our ongoing responsibility as stewards. We are told that even our descendants will dispossess nations and settle in their desolate cities. Isaiah 49:19–20 gives this warning: "Though you were ruined and made desolate and your land laid waste, now you will be too small for your people, and those who devoured you will be far away. The children born during your bereavement will yet say in your hearing, 'This place is too small for us; *give us more space to live in'*" (emphasis mine). We must realize that we are preparing ourselves and our next generation for the stewarding of that which is yet to come. Therefore, the boundaries and foundations that we are setting now will determine that which is still to take place.

The original mandate God gave Abraham in Genesis 2 was similar: to extend the blessing that he received to all the different peoples on the earth. Enlarging the tent, stretching the tent curtains, lengthening its cords and strengthening its stakes refers to the tabernacle, the place where the Lord dwelled among His people (see Exodus 35). Thus, this language is used in Isaiah to call us to prepare a place for the Lord in our land with an ever-increasing level of responsibility and care that God is entrusting to us. This sense of extension was paramount in the strategy of the Church in the early days of mission zeal, and the tent needs the same type of expansion today, since revival is coming!

The Good and Faithful Servant

As we learn from the parable of the talents (see Matthew 25:14–30), the master is thrilled with the good and faithful servant who undertakes wise investment of the property entrusted to him. Verse 29 is quite clear: "For everyone who has will be given more, and he will have an abundance. Whoever does not have, even what he has will be taken from him." Luke 12:48 says something similar: "From everyone who has been given much, much will be demanded; and from the one who has been entrusted with much, much more will be asked." This expectation that is placed upon the faithful servant is a critical part of learning how to steward and sustain authentic revival.

When revival comes to a community, every system of life in that community becomes subservient to the higher purposes of God. It is the mandate of the Body of Christ to ensure that the community enters into faithful stewardship of the Lord's presence. This type of stewardship is what Zechariah 8:3 refers to as the "City of Truth" or the "faithful city." A few verses later Zechariah offers sobering instruction in the importance of stewarding territory in a manner that brings the Lord honor and glory and draws others to us because they recognize that God is with us:

> This is what the LORD Almighty says: "Many peoples and the inhabitants of many cities will yet come, and the inhabitants of one city will go to another and say, 'Let us go at once to entreat the LORD and seek the LORD Almighty. I myself am going.' And many people and powerful nations will come to Jerusalem to seek the LORD Almighty and to entreat him." This is what the LORD Almighty says: "In those days ten men from all languages and nations will take firm hold of one Jew by the edge of his robe and say 'Let us go with you, because we have heard that God is with you'" (Zechariah 8:20–23).

To summarize, the Church has the responsibility of stewardship and guardianship over the land God entrusts to it. We must be vigilant and attentive to any issue of sin that could become a foothold for the enemy. We must care for, pray for and protect the leadership, their relationships, their decision-making and their families. We must nurture corporate prayer and continually seek God's developing vision and purpose for the city. We must be faithful with what has been entrusted to us, so that God can give us even more. Faithfully stewarding the territory ensures that the name and presence of the Lord will dwell forever in our midst (see 2 Chronicles 7:15–16).

There is another principle of stewardship that enables us to steward the territory and to ensure that the presence of the Lord is sustained in His reviving power. And this principle affects the entire Body of Christ! It is the principle of unity.

8

...

The Unity Principle

The greatest miracle of that day [Pentecost] was the transformation wrought in these waiting disciples. Their fire-baptism transformed them.

Samuel Chadwick

I find the words of Proverbs 11:14 more than challenging: "For lack of guidance a nation falls, but many advisers make victory sure." These words hold a sense of high expectation that when leaders in a nation come together under the sovereignty of God's power and direction, He is able to move that nation into its destiny. Ecclesiastes 4:12 gives insight into how this can take place: "Though one may be overpowered, two can defend themselves. A cord of three strands is not quickly broken." Furthermore, the well-known words of Matthew 18:19–20 give specific direction: "Again, I tell you that if two of you on earth agree about anything you ask for, it will be done for you by my Father in heaven. For where two or three come together in my name, there am I with them."

Jesus even goes so far as to say that when two or three come together in *His* name that He will be present! Clearly, something profound and powerful surrounds this whole subject of agreement and authority. Thus, we see that unity is one of the main attractors of God's presence.

Dislodging or Discouraging Revival

In almost every example of revival throughout history, at least a few people came together in the Lord's name and asked Him to visit their land. In researching information for this book, I visited Wales and the Hebrides Islands off the northwest coast of Scotland, two areas that have experienced fairly recent revival. In both locations I asked a number of people if they believed any one particular reason brought the revivals in their respective areas to an end. The answer I heard over and over again was that unity was lost due to denominationalism, jealousy and sometimes criticism, and this lack of unity then dislodged what had been developing among the people of God.

For whatever reason disunity exists or develops, once it is present it is almost impossible for the Body of Christ to speak into the heart of a city or nation with any real sense of authority or concern. In 1 Corinthians 1:10–17 Paul referred to the variety of divisions that existed in the church of his day. He quoted different people, who followed different leaders for one reason or another, and each spoke in the first person. That is, each one used the pronoun *I* rather than *we*, demonstrating individualism and resistance to working together. Paul was well aware of the fact that when human wisdom reigns, the cross of Christ is emptied of its power (see 1 Corinthians 1:17). Paul asked the people this searching question: "Is Christ divided?" (1 Corinthians 1:13).

Christ is not divided. He is all about unity. Recently I read some *Every Day with Jesus* Bible study notes that were produced by Crusade For World Revival in Farnham, England. The following words stood out to me:

> Sadly, this spirit lingers in the Church of Christ right up to this present day. One person made the following comment: "God has let down a rope from heaven for us to take hold of—that rope is Christ. But we have taken the end of that rope and unraveled it into strands. One group takes hold of a strand and builds a whole denomination around it. Each thinks he has the truth when all he may have is truths about the Truth—the truth in the rope, not the strand. And we will be surprised that when God pulls up the rope a lot of other people holding to their strands will come up too." The fragmentation of the Church, which has been split into so many factions and denominations, undermines our witness to the world we are trying to win. We must pray, work, and do all that we can in a practical way to heal these divisions in the Body of Christ.[1]

Even in revival itself, unity can become the focus of our choosing to relate with each other. If that is the end of our vision, we are going to be sadly discouraged. Working with city ministry initiatives all over the world, time and time again we find that an incorrect focus on unity alongside weak leadership almost inevitably results in a failed attempt at community transformation. Of course, in many ways, weak leadership is the product of a lack of unity, and a lack of unity is in itself a product of weak leadership! The focus of unity is found in the heart of God Himself.

Beauty in Unity

One of my favorite passages in Scripture is Matthew 4:18–22 in which Jesus calls some of His early disciples to follow Him. Two of these disciples, James and John, were found preparing their nets with their father. The Greek word for *preparing* is *katartizo,* which is a medical word meaning "to put back into proper alignment so that everything works according to design." Mending or preparing nets in this fashion also involves re-strengthening the strands so that the entire net is strong, thus correcting any weakness. When Jesus approached they were "preparing their nets"—that is, they were ensuring that the entire net was strong and they were correcting any weaknesses. This is a beautiful picture of what the Church must be doing when the presence of the Lord comes to dwell among us. We must be ensuring that our "nets" are strong and that there is no discord, disunity or dysfunction among us that may cause weakness.

The same word is used in Ephesians 4:12 as a means of explaining the purpose of the five-fold ministry gifts listed in the preceding verse. The function of these gifts is "to prepare God's people for works of service, so that the body of Christ may be built up." Here the word *katartizmon* is used with a sense of exhortation and encouragement in moving God's people into what He has prepared for them. If we are employing the ministry gifts in the way God intended, then we are like the fishermen preparing their nets. We are ensuring that the entire Body of Christ is strong, and we are correcting any weakness, so that the entire Church is prepared for the presence of the Lord.

But prior to giving this instruction, Paul instructs the Church to keep the unity of the Spirit (see Ephesians 4:3), since relational unity is what undergirds functional unity. Paul understood that we can be one in the spirit even if we do not all believe or function the same way.

In her book *Unity in the Spirit,* my friend Ruth Ruibal of Cali, Columbia, whom I mentioned in chapter 1, shares how the pastors of her city entered into a covenant of unity before the Lord. Her husband, Julio, a leader who longed to see the destiny of the Lord fulfilled in his city, had just been martyred. This sent a shock of disbelief throughout many Christian leaders in Cali. Ruth describes what then happened:

> The idea was to promise God, and each other, that we would work together in unity to see His purposes fulfilled in our land, and that nothing would be allowed to separate us—that we were one. Of course, I gave my consent and we embraced one another making that covenant. The presence of the Lord was so real that everyone could sense it. I believe that it was at this moment that we stepped from cooperation into unity. For me, this was one of the most important events in the history of Cali. In spite of our deep sorrow, there was also joy as we waited expectantly for what the Lord would do next. When there is sacrifice, God sends the fire.[2]

In chapter 2 of her book, Ruth explains the beauty of diversity, evident in the tribes of Israel. For example, Issachar had wisdom, Judah had the gift of praise and Dan was known for executing the judgments or justice of God. While each tribe had all the characteristics of God, each also was known for a specific characteristic that when brought alongside all the others gave "a more complete picture of the God served by the Israelites."[3] Ruth's own experience has taught her a powerful principle: ". . . True unity demands diversity; otherwise, it would be uniformity, not unity."[4]

Similarly, within each church, each community, each city and each nation, God has positioned something unique that when released reflects His higher purposes for all the peoples of the world. In so doing He has given the world a more complete picture of what He is like.

As the Church in the twenty-first century, we must be about the business of "preparing the nets." We must ensure that our Body is strong and without discord or weakness, and that we are utilizing each unique gift for the higher purposes of the Lord. In this way, the beauty of God's unifying Spirit is glorified and His power is made manifest.

Power in Unity

There is power in unity. This is why David refers to unity in Psalm 133 with such a sense of excitement and joy. When the people of God live together in this degree of unity, He can command His blessing (see verses 1–3).

In chapter 3, we reflected on John 17 and Jesus' desire for us to be in complete unity in the same way that He and the Father are one. This is the testimony that will convince the world that Jesus is who He says He is. With this understanding, the city churches, comprising all the wonderful varieties of congregations, can come together to form the prophetic mouthpiece of God in that place. Paul puts it this way: "May the God who gives endurance and encouragement give you a *spirit of unity* among yourselves as you follow Christ Jesus, so that with *one heart and mouth* you may glorify the God and Father of our Lord Jesus Christ. Accept one another, then, just as Christ accepted you, in order to bring praise to God" (Romans 15:5–7, emphasis mine).

Paul paints a beautiful picture of what happens when the power of unity is at work within the Body of Christ. When we are unified, we speak forth the mind of Christ with one voice embraced with rich diversity. At this point, God is able to sow His vision and His purpose into the members of His Body because they are sharing in one mind and one spirit. Such unity attracts God to any community.

Relational Unity Undergirds the Church

One of my favorite passages in the Bible is Judges 1, in which an evil king called Adoni-Bezek is confronted by two of the tribes of Israel. Seventy kings had tried to defeat Adoni-Bezek individually, and he had conquered them all. He even humiliated the vanquished kings by cutting off their thumbs and big toes—an act that is representative of the individual kings not being able to *grasp* the things of God or *stand* for the things of God. But when the tribes of Judah and Simeon decided to join together to take on this enemy, he was defeated and brought to justice.

Until the brothers came together, there was an imbalance of power and an inability to deal with the problem at hand. What a lesson and what an encouragement this passage is for the twenty-first century Church as we prepare to take on a myriad of giants who are trying to bring chaos and disorder to the world! Only in unity can we succeed—and only when we move from a formal type of cooperation into the type of spiritual unity that releases the power and authority of the Lord.

Matthew 18:18–20 directly addresses the power and authority that God bequeaths to His unified Church:

> "I tell you the truth, whatever you bind on earth will be bound in heaven, and whatever you loose on earth will be loosed in heaven. Again, I tell you that if two of you on earth agree about anything you ask for, it will be done for you by my Father in heaven. For where two or three come together in my name, there am I with them."

When agreement and the mind of Christ prevail within the Body of Christ, the will of the Father in heaven can be done on earth. As somebody once said, "As goes the Church, so goes the world." Whatever the Church models in her own life can become a living testimony to the rest of the world. It is helpful to remember that the Lord is coming back for His Bride, not a harem!

My good friend John Robb is director of prayer mobilization for World Vision International and also serves as international coordinator for the Great Commission Global Roundtable. I have had the privilege of serving with John on various international prayer initiatives throughout different parts of the world. I humorously refer to him as the Indiana Jones of prayer initiatives, and recently he showed me his Indiana Jones hat that he wears on certain prayer initiatives! In *The Peacemaking Power of Prayer,* a dynamite book that John co-authored with James A. Hill, he graphically describes what happened in the prayer initiatives that have taken place in recent years in Bosnia, Kosovo, Cambodia and Rwanda. On each occasion when the prayer initiative teams began to pray with the understanding and authority of Matthew 18, significant changes began to take place at the heart of each of these nations in the days that followed. The authors remind us of the phenomenal power of prayer:

> Secular media has largely omitted reporting on the role prayer has played in the great social and political transformations of our time, such as the fall of the Berlin Wall and reunification of Germany, the Romanian revolution and the overthrow of Ceaucescu, or the birth of the new South Africa. In all three of these cases, believers were actively praying for God's intervention and transformation during the times of conflict and social turmoil that preceded the positive changes that later occurred.[5]

When relational unity undergirds the life of the Church, Jesus' promise in John 14:13–14 is confirmed: "And I will do whatever you ask in my name, so that the Son may bring glory to the Father. You may ask me for anything in my name, and I will do it." Or, putting it another way, "nothing is impossible with God" (Luke 1:37). Relational unity is a powerful tool in our artillery, since it is as relevant in praying for an entire nation as it is for an individual.

No Room for Offense

The issue of offense is one of the subtlest yet most iniquitous means by which the enemy can destroy unity within the Body of Christ. In meetings of the Cali church leaders, various problems and issues between churches and pastors were resolved in a godly way. Writing of this, Ruth Ruibal makes a point that is so often misunderstood or overlooked by church leadership:

> "Unity" was a key word. These men of God on the Board frequently reminded each other of the covenant that they had made. They worked into the night to seek the mind of the Lord for the answers to vexing problems. More mature leaders would take a loss before letting a younger man become offended. There was a deliberate choice of unity.[6]

An issue of offense infiltrated a church I pastored many years ago. A good friend was serving as my senior elder for a season when I noticed that while I was preaching in Sunday services people began to look at their watches on an ever-increasing basis. I later found out that this elder friend had begun a competition in the church to see who could guess the length of my sermons most accurately. Shortly after that, I noticed people busying themselves with something that took up their attention following the conclusion of my sermons. On one occasion somebody came up and showed me the number "8" on a piece of paper. When I inquired what this was all about, I was told that my preaching received a mark of 8 on that particular

Sunday. I decided not to ask whether this was out of a scale of 10 or 20, but I very quickly found the source of this latest ecclesiastical game! It was my friend once again. I felt offended, and because I was offended, he became offended at me. Suddenly there was a break in our friendship and collegiality, and this led to a loss of loyalty. I could not trust him, and he did not want to trust me.

For some weeks this issue was left unaddressed, and it was slowly beginning to have an effect upon the church. I remember praying in my office and sensed the Holy Spirit telling me to call this man and invite him and his wife for dinner. When I mentioned this to my wife there was a slight pause on the other end of the phone, but I did believe this was the right thing to do. When I called with the invitation, my elder asked if there was any ulterior motive, and I said no. I said simply that I thought it was time for us to get together and it might be most appropriate to do this over a meal. We two couples finally met, and as we looked to each other for fellowship, the enemy suddenly lost his foothold and all measures of betrayal and offense were removed. Once the pastor and senior elder were reunited in their relationship with each other, a huge sigh of relief swept through our church body.

Why do people get offended with each other? Why do people get offended with Jesus? What was it that offended Absalom and led to his betrayal of David? Why was Cain so offended by Abel that he murdered him? People can feel offended because they are misunderstood or because they feel they are overlooked, or because greater recognition is given to other people's gifts and talents—such was the case between Cain and Abel and their respective offerings to the Lord. Many people in churches take offense because they are not given a certain position or recognition they are seeking. They may be looking for a more recognized level of responsibility, and lack of recognition seeds the root of offense in their hearts. People may feel offended for many reasons, and Jesus said, "Many will be offended, will betray one another, and will hate one another" (Matthew 24:10, NKJV).

With sobering words, Campbell McAlpine discusses this verse in his book *Explaining Loyalty, Betrayal and Offense*:

> In this statement the Lord gave one of the basic reasons why people became disloyal: being offended. It is evident that Judas Iscariot became an offended man; offended because things were not working out as he had thought they would. The super earthly kingdom was not going to be established. . . . He may even have been offended with Peter, James and John because of their intimate fellowship with Jesus, and His with them. Whatever the reason, the seed had been planted, and the consequence of being offended is betrayal. The cause of all of offense is pride, and is evidenced by criticism, judgment, resentment, vindictiveness, self-defense and self-pity; all resulting in self-inflicted wounds. There are two dangers which we should all try and avoid: giving offense and taking offense. The truth is, there are so many offended Christians in the Church today; so many hurting people. The tragedy is that no offended Christian can ever be truly loyal.[7]

Perhaps Judas was offended because he felt Jesus was moving too slowly and that his betrayal would cause Jesus to act with greater authority. Whatever the case may be, Judas obviously had not learned that people do not change Jesus, but rather Jesus changes people.

This was a key element in the unity developed among Ruth Ruibal's colleagues. The more mature leaders were conscientious in their desire to maintain unity at all costs and chose not to be offended by younger, more immature leaders who were trying to exert their influence. They knew that giving offense only leads to hurt and betrayal, and that only Jesus changes people.

It is easy to become offended if people are entrenched in religious traditions and find it hard to see beyond their comfortable ecclesiastical wineskins. We are living in a day and age when God is shaking man-made foundations and leading the Church back to the early foundations and boundaries He established. Only in returning to His ways can intimacy be released in our relationships with the Lord and become the means by which revival enters our midst. As McAlpine so simply puts it:

> How many times do church constitutions take precedence over the teaching of the word of God, when sentimentality becomes more important than spirituality? Thank God for all the good traditions of the past, and for all that He has done in, and for, His church, but if we do anything which is not originated by God, it will not be energized by God.[8]

When offense leads to betrayal, which in turn leads to hatred, a root of bitterness is sown that can defile an individual, a church, and even a city and a nation. God's presence cannot dwell where roots of bitterness are sown. This is one of the major reasons for the disintegration of a community or city that is in transformation. Ponder these penetrating words God gives to His people, "Then I will go back to my place until they admit their guilt. And they will seek my face; in their misery they will earnestly seek me. Come, let us return to the Lord. He has torn us to pieces but he will heal us" (Hosea 5:15–6:1). If we are people who are offended with each other, or even with the Lord, then He will return to "His place."

Only recently I heard of an assembly of people numbering in the thousands who were praying together on a regular basis in a community here in North America. Just as I was about to research what was bringing these people together, I discovered that the whole movement had all but disintegrated and many were left disillusioned and dismayed. I also am aware of another large city where seventy to eighty pastors were meeting regularly for prayer. This ministerial gathering had been increasing gradually over the last two or three years, until suddenly it all but disintegrated.

Something similar happened in these two situations: The issue of offense, disloyalty, lack of trust and individualism penetrated what God was trying to accomplish! When the people of God start praying and meeting with each other on a regular basis, the enemy becomes concerned. He then uses even our greatest strength against us, because the place of our strength can also be our greatest vulnerability. That is the place we most often leave unprotected. We must never forget that the enemy goes about like a prowling lion.

When stewarding revival, attitude and reaction are significant monitors of the principle of unity. Inevitably, opposition will occur at times since revival in the Church always involves change, and change results in a variety of emotions—suspicion, anger, indifference and even jealousy! Often, I have had the privilege of sharing in conferences with Steve Fry. When addressing this issue of reaction, he cites the example of one church fellowship that prayed for revival, but when revival finally came, another totally different fellowship—one that had been spiritually dead—received the fire! The praying church's reaction was, "That's not fair, since we've been the ones praying for revival!" But the Lord indicated that He *did* answer their prayers and chose an area that would most clearly reveal His reviving power at work! In this situation, it was important for the praying church to maintain a right attitude toward the one where revival started, so that unity could prevail and the Holy Spirit could expand this revival and thus permeate the entire community.

Fish says, "A patient, kind and prayerful spirit toward those who are in opposition will actually perpetuate revival."[9] This is the spirit that strengthens and matures relational unity, that develops trust and friendship even when we are not always in agreement on the way things should be done! The Lord told us to love one another. It is, therefore, important to acknowledge this to one another when we are offended. The depth by which we love the Lord whom we have not seen is determined by the degree to which we love those whom we have seen (see 1 John 4:20).

Proverbs 18:19 reminds us: "An offended brother is more unyielding than a fortified city." Perhaps this is why Paul says so graphically in Ephesians 4:3 that we are to make every effort to keep the unity of the Spirit through the bond of peace and through the love of Christ. This is how we prohibit the enemy of God's people from gaining a foothold; peace and love are also vital for maintaining the unity that attracts God's attention whenever His people come together in His name.

Arise, O Lord God

I love these words from 2 Chronicles 6:41: "Now arise, O LORD God, and come to your resting place, you and the ark of your might." Just think about that for a moment—the living God Himself arising at *our* request and coming to His resting place in our midst because He promised that when two or three people come together in His name, He will be there among them. It was this power of unity and relationship that enabled the Son to do the work of the Father. As a result He was able to minister with a power of compassion that opened the eyes of the people to the knowledge of the Kingdom of God.

This is also our mandate. Revival can be dislodged and transformation can be dismissed when the people of God cease to walk, work and worship together as the Body of Christ. But when relational unity prevails, a divine cohesiveness forms among the local church fellowships and leads to what is known as the city church. At this point, the Church once again becomes the prophetic voice of the Lord in the land and the compassion of the Lord is released upon the frailty of society.

9

...

Is Everything A.O.K.?

Revival and evangelism, although closely linked, are not to be confounded. Revival is an experience in the Church; evangelism is one expression of the Church.

Paul S. Rees

The whole subject of acts of kindness (A.O.K.) is one of the most fascinating yet misunderstood principles that can both prepare a community for revival and enable a community to sustain revival on an ongoing basis. In its simplest definition, *compassion* means "to suffer with another person, having pity or sympathy for his plight." The Greek language has a fascinating word for *compassion—splagchnizomai—*which refers to the entire inner being of a person yearning with pity and sympathy to bring relief to those in need. True compassion is an intense depth of concern moving God's people to respond to the plight of humanity.

C. Peter Wagner makes an interesting comment in his book *Revival! It Can Transform Your City*:

> Unfortunately, very few churches or Christian organizations in the inner city—or in the suburbs for that matter—have well-developed ministries of personal deliverance. Many parachurch ministries focus on the inner cities, and I have read the descriptive literature distributed by several of them. They are tooled to provide medical or dental service, to give clothing to the homeless, to manage soup kitchens, to offer legal assistance, to help people find jobs, to tutor school children, to hold Bible studies, to staff day-care centers, to finance small businesses, to run crisis pregnancy centers, to play midnight basketball, and to do many other good things. However, I have yet to find a brochure advertising that their ministry casts out demons.[1]

The activities Wagner lists as typical of parachurch ministries are examples of acts of kindness or compassion. The point he makes about casting out demons as part of that compassion is an important one. Is it not possible to focus on both the usual acts of kindness as well as personal deliverance in order to steward the presence of the Most High God? We will ponder the answer to this question later in this chapter.

The Compassion of Jesus

Many times in the Gospels Jesus was moved with compassion. He subsequently ministered to the people in ways specific to their individual needs. His ministry resulted in people being healed, fed, clothed and delivered from demons. For example,

> Jesus went through all the towns and villages, teaching in their synagogues, preaching the good news of the king-

dom and healing every disease and sickness. When he saw the crowds, he had compassion on them, because they were harassed and helpless, like sheep without a shepherd. Then he said to his disciples, "The harvest is plentiful but the workers are few. Ask the Lord of the harvest, therefore, to send out workers into his harvest field."

Matthew 9:35–38

Jesus' life was a perfect, authentic demonstration of the nature of the Kingdom of God. Verse 36 says that Jesus looked at the people, saw their needs and had *compassion* on them, since He recognized that life had not been fair to them. He traveled from one place to another teaching, preaching and healing—in other words, ministering to the needs of the people. When He was among the people, their needs were met. In the same way, when revival happens and God's presence comes to dwell among the Church today, the Church must have the same compassion and minister to the needs of the people. Such ministering is a normal outworking of the Kingdom of God among us.

In verse 37, Jesus says that the harvest is ready. The harvest to which He refers is the fruit that comes out of authentic revival. In other words, there is a very close connection between revival, harvest and the compassion of Jesus that operates before and after revival happens.

Jesus did not even allow His own needs to prevent Him from ministering to the people: "When Jesus heard what had happened, he withdrew by boat privately to a solitary place. Hearing of this, the crowds followed him on foot from the towns. When Jesus landed and saw a large crowd, he had compassion on them and healed their sick" (Matthew 14:13–14). Even though Jesus needed to be in a solitary place, the people were drawn to the power of the Kingdom of God, and as a result Jesus looked on them with compassion and ministered to their needs accordingly.

Scripture is full of references to God's compassionate heart. David was well aware of the compassionate nature of God: "But you, O Lord, are a compassionate and gracious God, slow to anger, abounding in love and faithfulness" (Psalm 86:15). And Peter said, "Finally, all of you, live in harmony with one another; be sympathetic, love as brothers, be compassionate and humble" (1 Peter 3:8).

Matthew 20:29–34 gives a wonderful account of two blind men by the roadside who were not able to see all the activity taking place as Jesus left Jericho. The cry from their hearts and mouths drowned out the noise of the crowd: "Lord, Son of David, have mercy on us" (verse 30). Jesus turned and called them, asking what they wanted. They said that they wanted their sight. So out of compassion, Jesus touched their eyes and healed them.

Jesus was so moved with compassion that the power of the Kingdom of God needed to be released from within Him in order to meet the needs of mankind. The compassion of Jesus that He modeled for His people is a powerful key to understanding the nature of revival. As we have discussed, revival is a return to that life of intimacy with the presence of God, who is then able to work in and through us to permeate every aspect of society. In order to bear such fruitfulness, we must have the compassion of Jesus. He knew the harvest was ready and waiting to be gathered. His concern was, would His people be prepared to respond to the needs?

The Witness of Compassion in Revival

Compassion can be a powerful evangelical witness. In her book *Unity in the Spirit*, Ruth Ruibal describes what happened when a group of people sought practical, compassionate ways in which to serve their city:

The Ministers' Association once asked the mayor how the church might help serve our city. One problem was with garbage collection in a certain area of the city, so we offered our help. In coordination with the city government, 1,500 believers gathered on a Saturday morning to collect garbage—40 tons of it. In the process 500 people came to know the Lord as their Savior! We didn't realize that it would be a city-church evangelistic garbage team! We discovered that service opens doors in a wonderful way to win people to Jesus.[2]

Recently, a church leader told me of a similar situation in which hundreds of Christians began to address some of the more visible needs of their community in Canada. They cleaned the windows of offices and stores. They cleaned office restrooms and back alleys. They picked up prescriptions for seniors and drove them to do their shopping. Reactions from the city included suspicious amusement and curiosity, as well as amazement for the quality of work that was undertaken voluntarily. Questions regarding their motivation were answered humbly. The real test came when the Church invited the community to a celebration in the local stadium—and the place was filled! Such "random acts of kindness," as these church activities are termed, establish a physical and tangible statement that the Church wants to care for its community! This is compassion at work on one level, preparing the city for a deeper level.

However, it is also establishing something else. The Church is making a prophetic statement into the spiritual realm that they are prepared to remove all the spiritual debris connected with the life of the city—to remove the obstructions, impediments and obstacles—and then to invite the Lord to come and rest in that place. This is the power of compassion at work in both the physical and spiritual realms. As Ruth Ruibal's group and the Canadian church found out, the moment the Body of Christ begins to activate the compassion of Jesus at any level—even by removing garbage—the spiritual eyes of the people in that community can be opened to the reality of the Kingdom of God in their midst. It is a practical and powerful way to show people the light of the Gospel at work, and to condition their spiritual eyesight for a divine disclosure (see 2 Corinthians 4:4).

When the compassion of Jesus is released through the Body of Christ, it is simply amazing what God is able to do. In Cali, Colombia, the traditional Christmas celebration is called the *Feria*, and it is noted for debauchery, promiscuity and other social problems. It is quite similar to the Mardi Gras in New Orleans or Carnavale in Rio de Janeiro. Ruth Ruibal tells how the mayor of Cali issued an invitation to the area Christian church to participate in the festivities with Christian input, both in terms of the music and the message. Thus, on an occasion when most Christians normally would leave the city, the city instead was asking Christians to participate—on their terms!—in one of the city's celebrations of life. Ruth describes the result of that participation:

> That Christmas *Feria*, for the first time in the history of Cali, brought the gospel message to crowds of people who had come with a very different agenda. The whole atmosphere of the *Feria* changed. Wild partying was mixed with a message of truth and seriousness. . . . We weren't comfortable dealing with a situation like the *Feria*, but we were learning. The important thing is that the Lord's name was glorified and many did come to know the Lord as their Savior.[3]

The witness of compassion can move even authorities to ask for help and involvement from the people of God.

Many years ago when I was pastoring, we asked Graham Kerr—known for his earlier days as the Galloping Gourmet but now a vibrant Christian—and his wife, Treena, to lead one of our church camps. It was a wonderful occasion, never to be forgotten, and our camp theme was A.O.K. (Acts of Kindness). Graham made a point I have never forgotten—that even the slightest act of kindness is a witness to the power of the Kingdom of God at work in our midst. Jesus puts it this way: "Whatever you did for one of the least of these brothers of mine, you did for me" (Mathew 25:40).

Cities throughout the United States, Canada and elsewhere in the world have developed intercessory strategies that are steeped in hands-on compassion. The intercessors themselves actually participate in "hands-on ministry," clothing the poor and feeding the hungry, and even visiting those in prison. At the same time, they are praying into the roots of dishevelment and impoverishment that have placed these people into such bondage and turmoil. Many ministries such as The Salvation Army, Youth With A Mission, Mercy Ships and World Vision, to name but a few, are wonderfully humanitarian and reach out to meet the needs that are so often missed or ignored by the Body of Christ at large.

However, we are referring to something much deeper. Acts of kindness can welcome revival into a city, and they can sustain the reviving power of God in that city on an ongoing basis. Billy Graham has been aware of this all throughout his ministry. I recall a visit he made to Vancouver, Canada, several years ago. Before undertaking the first night of his evangelistic mission, he was found taking food to the local Food Bank, and talking and ministering with the homeless and the hungry. He knew that acts of kindness served as tangible witnesses to the Kingdom of God loving these people. How better to draw people to the Lord than to serve as the hands of Christ?

The Power of Compassion in Revival

When revival comes to a community, it normally high-lights the needs of the people who live in that place. The compassion of God literally pours into—and out from— His Body, and people are wonderfully delivered, set free, filled with the Holy Spirit and established in a whole new lifestyle. Their desire is to continue in that new lifestyle from one degree of glory to another. But sustaining revival requires the "hands-on" involvement of people who become spiritual caretakers of their city. When that sense of compassion or care wanes or is lost, the activity of the Lord Jesus becomes less apparent.

Some months ago at a conference, I was informed of a group of young people who had developed a unique way of evangelizing people in the downtown sector of their city. The Psychic Fair was coming to town, and while most churches told their young people not to go near it, this one particular church instead began preparing their young people to enter "the lion's den." The church spent a great deal of time teaching the young people about intercession, spiritual warfare and accountability. They taught them how to walk and live in the power of the Holy Spirit, how to recognize the voice of the Lord, and how to know when God might reveal certain issues. Also, the church's seasoned intercessors were praying for these young people.

The Psychic Fair arrived and this youth group set up a "Prophetic Stall" right in the middle of it. As people came to have tarot cards read for them and have their fortunes told and use crystals in an occult fashion, they passed by this Prophetic Stall and asked the young people what they were doing there. Their response was this: "We would like to give you a word from the Lord!" People thought this was rather unusual but innovative, and often said that they would be open for receiving any "revelation" coming their way—bear in mind they had come to a psychic fair.

As these young people prayed for the individuals, God revealed various issues about their lives. Several times the passers-by were so shocked that they asked, "How did you know this? Where did you get your information? Does God really know about this?" On several occasions the individuals went to the church that had sent out these young messengers of the Lord, and were introduced into the Kingdom of God! Several other churches in the city now participate in this activity, ensuring that care and protection are placed over the young people at all times and that the teenagers are very cognizant of the boundaries the Lord positions around them.

On another occasion, several churches taught their intercessory youth groups how to go on a "prayer walk." They learned to wait outside homes while God gave them insight into what to pray for the people who lived there. They would then go to the doors and say that they were from the local city church and offer, "We just want you to know that we are praying for you because we sense somebody is sick here" or "somebody needs work" or "there is some problem or concern, and we would like to pray for you." People were both shocked and amazed that young people would come to the door wanting to pray for them—and even seemed to be aware of their most pressing needs! A follow-up visit would be made two or three weeks later, often to find that many direct answers to prayer had occurred. The people they visited began to attend the local churches and commit their lives to Christ.

There is no such thing as a "Junior Holy Spirit," and children are among the purest of vessels the Lord can use to discharge the power of His Kingdom. Whether these communities knew it or not, very powerful acts of kindness were at work in their midst addressing spiritual and physical issues in a somewhat unique, yet strategic and practical manner. The young people in these youth groups served as powerful spiritual caretakers of their cities.

Is Everything A.O.K.?

All of the examples in this chapter simply scratch the surface of what the compassion of Jesus really involves. The compassion of Jesus means ensuring that the needs of people are met—be it clothing for the homeless, soup kitchens, legal assistance, crisis pregnancy centers and so on. However, whatever the act of kindness may be, if the Lord has called us to undertake it as a demonstration of the Kingdom of God in that community, then almost undoubtedly we will touch the lives, minds and hearts of the people who live in that place. Such is the power of an act of kindness that is immersed in the power of the Holy Spirit and that demonstrates the authenticity of the Kingdom of God as it invades the kingdom of man.

So let us answer the question I posed concerning the words of C. Peter Wagner at the beginning of this chapter. Wagner has challenged us with a serious spiritual principle, and I believe that the ministries of "hands-on organizations" *can* meet practical needs while also casting out demons. In fact, I believe this is crucial to sustaining revival. When revival comes to our cities, acts of kindness must involve a higher caliber of activity than ever before. This was the way of Jesus, this was the modeling of Jesus and this was the compassion of Jesus that He bequeathed to us in the power of the Holy Spirit. Revivals often end too soon because the activity of the Body of Christ is no longer stewarding the compassion of Christ in a way that opens up the eyes, ears, minds, hearts and hands of people to receive what God wants to give them.

Consider what potential acts of kindness are waiting to be discovered in *your* city. The harvest is waiting. How deep is *your* compassion?

10

...

Establishing Watchmen

Our praying, however, needs to be pressed and pursued
with an energy that never tires, a persistency that will not
be denied, and a courage that never fails.

E. M. Bounds

If we want to see our cities through the eyes of the Lord,
if we want to be moved with compassion and respond
accordingly, then it is time to make sure that watchmen
are fully involved and aware of all that is taking place. The
role of the watchmen is critical when it comes to stewarding the presence of the Lord.

Two passages in Scripture related to watchmen are especially challenging to me in my personal prayer life. The
first is Isaiah 62:6–7: "I have posted watchmen on your
walls, O Jerusalem; they will never be silent day or night.
You who call on the LORD, give yourselves no rest, and
give him no rest till he establishes Jerusalem and makes

her the praise of the earth." The second passage is Luke 18:6–8: "And the Lord said, 'Listen to what the unjust judge says. And will not God bring about justice for his chosen ones, who cry out to him day and night? Will he keep putting them off? I tell you, he will see that they get justice, and quickly. However, when the Son of Man comes, will he find faith on the earth?'"

These two passages indicate God's intention for us as His people of prayer and perseverance. In Isaiah 62, the watchmen are expected never to be quiet in their call and ministry, and neither are they to give the Lord any rest until He fulfills His purpose and fullness in their midst. Similarly, in Luke 18 the Lord encourages us that when we cry out to Him day and night He will listen to us, and He will invoke justice. This in itself will be a testimony to the degree of faith in our lives.

Standing in the Gap

In every authentic revival that we have researched, a common denominator is persistent prayer. In all cases, God's people were willing to pay the price on behalf of others in order for the Lord to visit their land. They were willing to stand in the gap.

Ezekiel 22:30 speaks of God's search for those who are willing to do so: "I looked for a man among them who would build up the wall and stand before me in the gap on behalf of the land so I would not have to destroy it, but I found none." God is looking for someone to "stand in the gap," a phrase that comes from a Hebrew law court metaphor. Used in this instance, God wants His people to "stand in the gap" on behalf of the land so that the judgment and curse upon the land can be removed, and His whole measure of destiny and healing can be released. We are called to be His advocates and to pray for order and restoration to replace disorder and destruction. As His advocates, we take the position figuratively of placing one hand on His head and one hand on the head of the problem, and we bring the two together so that disorder is removed and order is established. When the Church is positioned in this place of responsibility and is willing both to address any form of disorder on the land and to pray in the destiny of the Lord, it then can speak forth the word and counsel of the Lord with real authority and authenticity. Once we have served as His advocates through prayer and God's purposes are back in a place of divine order, then the Church can become an effective prophetic mouthpiece in the heart of society.

Standing in the gap, or engaging in persistent prayer, is what the image of the threshing floor is all about. As we discussed briefly in chapter 2, the threshing floor is a biblical metaphor used to describe the meeting place between God and man—the place where God threshes out the chaff from the seed of mankind. It is a place for both separation and celebration! After the oxen stumbled at the threshing floor while pulling the cart upon which the Ark of the Covenant was placed (see 1 Chronicles 13; 2 Samuel 6), issues had to be addressed before the presence of the Lord could be returned—that is, the divine order had to be restored. Another example of the threshing floor as a metaphor in Scripture is the account of Ruth going to Boaz. Following her mother-in-law's instructions, she went to Boaz at the threshing floor, positioning herself at his feet while he slept. When he awoke he would lose no time in making Ruth his bride. Ruth is a model for the Church to follow, posturing herself with humility and positioning herself on the threshing floor, waiting for the return of the Bridegroom. She had to remove her widow's dress and put on a bridal gown!

Currently, many books are available that give excellent teaching on intercessory prayer. Although we do recognize that intercessory prayer is a condition for lasting revival, we need to look at this subject in greater depth. Our focus here is not simply on the need for persistent, expectant prayer; it is on the fact that when such prayer loses momentum and vision, revival is threatened. God's people must continue to come to the threshing floor and cry out to Him, so that they can sound the alarm when the enemy tries to rob or steal, or when the Lord calls His people to attention. Praying for revival is only the first step. Beyond that, we must be aware of the heightened responsibility of *ongoing* prayer that is required to maintain the Lord's visitation.

Increased Territory Means Increased Responsibility

As we addressed in chapter 7, revival means a widening of the tent curtains. If the tent curtains are going to be stretched wide (see Isaiah 54:2) then God also extends the territory He assigns to us—and this means increased responsibility. Paul says,

> We, however, will not boast beyond proper limits, but will confine our boasting to the field God has assigned to us, a field that reaches even to you. . . . Our hope is that, as your faith continues to grow, our area of activity among you will greatly expand, so that we can preach the gospel in the regions beyond you.
>
> 2 Corinthians 10:13, 15–16

This subject of increased responsibility is vital to understanding how watchmen can effectively steward revival.

When the presence of the Lord comes into an area with reviving power, any remaining work of the enemy comes to light quickly. Issues of fear, uncertainty, intimidation, ignorance and unbelief are common issues that must be identified and prayed for right away. Immediately the tents of the watchmen are expanded, and they are required to pray for the entire community with a *greater* sense of responsibility.

In chapter 3 we looked at the subject of persevering leadership, and this is a very important subject to understand in terms of intercessory prayer. The watchmen must cover the leaders in the church, the leaders in industry and politics, those involved in education—indeed, anyone who is in any way at all involved in the leadership of the community. Unless our leaders are prayed for and protected, it will be all too easy for them to grow weary in the tasks appointed to them. Everything involved with the life of these people—the leaders themselves, their families, their local church congregations, their eldership, their health, finances and travel—need to be covered in prayer constantly. The relationships among the leaders also must be carefully watched and guarded so that no jealousy, anger or offense is permitted to go unaddressed. And as the circle of leadership increases, many more needs will arise that must be covered in prayer.

The term *increased territory* also means an increased expectation in ministry. I often challenge local church fellowships with this comment: "Many of you would probably enjoy having your congregation doubled in size within two weeks. However, would you be able to care for double the problems, and double the issues and double the needs, and double the responsibility that will be placed upon you pastorally in this church?" It is a reflective, but sobering question. Even now we need to be about the business of preparing the way for what is to come.

In order to steward revival correctly and carefully, even the watchmen themselves must be prayed for, cared for and trained for increasing areas of responsibility. Indeed, the training of new watchmen is vital if we are to pass the baton with a sense of responsibility and denominational collegiality. As the territory entrusted to us increases, so must the number of watchmen who are being trained to keep watch over God's stewardship day and night. In addition, local church fellowships should make their watchmen available to look after not just their own needs, but also the needs of other local churches and the needs of the entire city.

The principle of expanded tents is simple: To those to whom much is given, much more will be expected!

The Rhythms of the City

Watchmen are given responsibility for at least seven major areas of activity in every city and community. The first is, of course, the care of the city church, composed of all the various denominations. Each local fellowship begins praying for all the other fellowships. Then various intercessors who represent the city church are given collective authority within the city. This prayer constitutes the prophetic voice in the community. When the Church is listening to the Lord collectively, then the response is far quicker when the alarm is sounded. When the unity principle is at work in the life of the Church and collective watchmen are established, then if one church fellowship hurts or comes under any form of attack or assault, the rest of the church fellowships also will be affected and respond accordingly.

The next area of responsibility entrusted to the watchmen concerns those involved in the city's legal life— police personnel, security personnel, lawyers and judges. When the church of the land prays for the law of the land, honesty and integrity can infiltrate the life of that community.

Third, the watchmen take responsibility for the business sector. When each city church fellowship takes on prayerful responsibility for the businesses in their vicinity—praying for and caring for members of management, employees and even shareholders—the Lord is given the right of entrance into the marketplace through the prophetic voice of His people. When corruption is exposed and removed from the business world, then even our economy can experience the degree of lasting fruitfulness promised in Genesis 1:28.

Fourth, the watchmen are also given responsibility for praying into the political arena. When those in authority over us become subservient to the higher authority of the Lord Jesus Christ, it makes an enormous difference in the way the future of the land is shaped. For example, in Fiji and Uganda the ruling political parties have established new government positions dealing with the issues of reconciliation and integrity. Even in these early stages, such changes are having a significant effect upon the quality of life in these and other such nations.

Fifth, the watchmen have responsibility for those involved in the community's education. Each generation is responsible for the next generation, and one of the reasons revival is not sustained is because it does not affect the education curriculum in our communities! Watchmen have an enormous effect on both schools and colleges and can remain attentive to the development of any curriculum that is intended to influence children in a manner opposite God's Word. Similarly, educators who are prayed for regularly often testify to a greater sense of courage and freedom in imparting godly principles in what they teach and share. I know of schools that previously had closed the door on anything to do with the Church but suddenly reopened their doors to prayer, Bible teaching and the development of vibrant Christian student unions. Why? The intercessors were at work!

Sixth, the watchmen have responsibility for medical personnel and facilities. In the news these days one often hears about conflict in local communities between medical personnel and the government. The enemy quite simply loves to cause controversy, irritation and alienation between the officers of the city and the people of the land. As local churches adopt the hospitals, doctors, nurses and other medical facilities and personnel in their respective cities, the Lord is given greater freedom in establishing His sovereignty as the Great Physician in that city.

Finally, watchmen are given responsibility for praying over the media and entertainment industries—television, radio, cinema, sports and any other form of entertainment. When their lives come under the authority of Christ, people involved in these areas can exert a significant influence over a city. Furthermore, Christians involved in these activities need constant prayer because of the nature of the work they are doing and the tough issues they face.

Other areas exist, but these seven are the main areas of responsibility for church watchmen. They require commitment and willingness to become as actively involved in sustainable prayer as necessary until a breakthrough or noticeable change occurs. Stewarding revival, therefore, involves the continual covering of these areas in prayer along with the training of new watchmen while both the territory and responsibility increase.

Festering Footholds

In chapter 6 we addressed recurring footholds of sin, and in chapter 7 we looked at the importance of stewarding the territory. In caring for the territory, watchmen have to be vigilant when it comes to the subject of festering footholds.

Not long ago I had the privilege of working with an international ministry organization to pray over some new land given to them for ministry purposes. In previous years, this property had been under spiritual siege, and all four categories of sin that defile land—idolatry, immorality, bloodshed and broken covenants—had taken place there. When this Christian organization was given access to the territory, they initiated a great deal of productive prayer.

During my time working with the leadership, one of the things I noted was that the property seemed to be full of occult paraphernalia. Initially it looked harmless, but closer inspection revealed some of the many methods that occult and New Age practitioners use in order to win back lost territory. The enemy does not like to lose territory! He will use any means at his disposal to maintain his foothold so that it festers among God's people. Indeed, the leadership told me about ongoing domestic issues pertaining to illness, jealousy, fear and decision-making.

We began to engage in significant prayer and prophetic acts using salt, water and oil. The shofar was blown at all corners of the land, and a complete cleanup of all suspicious debris was undertaken. A sense of the majesty and presence of God began to come upon this vast property.

Only a few days later, two carloads of people arrived at the property and asked if they could simply stay on the property and pray. As it turned out, these people were affiliated with one of the world's most renowned New Age centers and had come to meditate upon the land. They knew that something in the spiritual realm had been stolen away from them, and they wanted that power restored. The ministry refused their request to come on the land and immediately alerted the intercessors. The leadership surveyed the territory to see if these people had left any fetishes or telltale articles that would have given them a spiritual entry point. The property was under siege by the enemy because he wanted it returned, and this siege required immediate action on the part of the ministry organization. They were not about to relinquish this hard-won territory and, if anything, the experience only served to strengthen the ministry's resolve to serve as God's steward.

As this experience indicates, it is important to work with trained watchmen who can sense what is going on in the spiritual realm and understand and interpret its effect on the physical realm. I shared with these people the importance of raising a canopy of prayer during the day—a type of prayer that protects all who come and go from that place and prohibits anybody from entering with an ulterior motive. I also showed them the importance of sealing off the property at night in the name of Christ and through the Blood of Christ, asking for angels to be in and through every building and upon every part of the land at all times. In this way, the enemy is prevented from maintaining any festering footholds. When watchmen undertake this on a daily basis in the power of the Holy Spirit—and not simply as a daily ritual—they release on a consistent basis the authority and power of the Lord Jesus in, around and upon His people. Then, when revival comes, it will be recognized, welcomed and stewarded.

Walking the Beat

As a young boy in Scotland I was always interested in the local policemen who regularly walked up and down their assigned territories. They called this "walking the beat." What they were doing was, in fact, looking out for any unusual change in their community. Putting it another way, they were looking for suspicious "contours of change."

Whenever any form of spiritual breakthrough takes place in a community or city, watchmen must be assigned to care for that new area—especially in the days following the actual ministry initiative. Doing so involves "walking the beat" in a spiritual sense, looking for suspicious contours of change in the spiritual realm that may be observable within the physical realm. Indeed, what we see taking place around us in the physical realm is very often a reflection of what is going on in the spiritual realm, and for this reason we must be able to see and think with the eyes and mind of Christ.

When watchmen undertake any form of such spiritual reconnaissance, they should do it with a sense of godly cognizance—that is, the Lord Himself in the power of the Holy Spirit must lead and guide them, directing them into all truth. When issues take place in the physical realm that cause suspicion and concern, and watchmen are already familiar with their beat, they are able to pray with much greater insight and authority over whatever may be trying to assault the Lord's people or His city.

It is also important to recognize that God wants His watchmen to be praying the prayers that He calls us to declare in His name. As we read in Ezekiel 3:17, "Son of man, I have made you a watchman for the house of Israel; *so hear the word I speak and give them warning from me*" (emphasis mine). God wants us to pray as *He* wants us to pray. He desires that we pray for His purposes. In order to know His purposes, the intercessor must be familiar with the beat, must listen to the Lord and watch what He reveals, and then must respond accordingly. Although the intensity of prayer goes through various seasons depending on what is taking place in the community at any one time, the need for vigilance never comes to an end.

The Result of Vigilant Watchmen

When revival comes to our cities, we have a heightened responsibility to keep watch both day and night, in season and out of season, never forgetting that a spiritual battle is fought continually for the lives of the people of God. We must not give God any rest until He establishes His purposes in the lives of His people and makes their city the praise of the earth. Through persistent, prevailing prayer the tent curtains can be stretched wide, the cords lengthened and the stakes strengthened. The presence of the Lord can then be stewarded and extended, and the Lord will have come to His resting place.

11

...

Guarding the Gates

Apostolic preaching is not marked by its beautiful diction, or literary polish, or cleverness of expression, but operates in demonstration of the Spirit and of power.

Arthur Wallis

In learning how to maintain the presence of God we have looked at the importance of persevering leadership, prevailing prayer, the fear of the Lord and intimacy with Him, ensuring no compromise is made over the issue of sin, stewarding the territory, the unity principle, acts of kindness based on the compassion of Jesus, and the necessity for establishing, maintaining and extending the role of watchmen. Similar to the role of watchmen is the role of godly gatekeepers.

How do gatekeepers differ from watchmen? Who are they, what do they do and what part do they play in welcoming God into a community that stewards His presence?

Identifying the Gatekeepers

Several books focus on the subject of gatekeepers, trying to determine from Scripture who they are and what their function involves. In most of today's church leadership circles, gatekeepers are regarded as representatives of city, regional, national and international levels. They represent the offices of clergy and pastors, members of the legal and security professions, politicians, educators, economists, health officials, media personnel and other key members in the indigenous community. While not every leader in these fields will always be regarded as a gatekeeper, there are those who are given specific God-given convocation and influence within their respective jurisdictions. They are affirmed or voted in by those they represent and who called them to fill this role. As far as their function is concerned, gatekeepers are people who protect, define, guard, decide, discern, direct, govern, permit or deny; in general, they are administrators of some fairly substantial authority within their area of responsibility.

In seeking to understand the role of the gatekeeper in modern-day ministry, it is helpful to examine scriptural examples of gatekeepers. First Chronicles 9:17 describes gatekeepers who were stationed at certain places around and within a city. Some were responsible for guarding the thresholds of the tent, while others guarded the entrance to the dwelling of the Lord. First Chronicles 9:22 indicates that all of these were positions of trust given to them by David and Samuel. Verse 27 further explains that these people would spend the night stationed around the house of God, guarding it, and they would open it in the morning with a key entrusted to their care. Similarly, 1 Chronicles 26 refers to the varying roles of the gatekeepers and their families, such as responsibility for the Temple and the storehouse.

In the early days of city development, the gateway into a city or a particular reference point, such as the Temple, was a place denoting responsibility and authority. For example, in Genesis 19:1, the angels arriving at Sodom in the evening found Lot sitting in the gateway of the city. More than likely, Lot was a member of Sodom's ruling council. It would have made sense for him to be there, since the gateways served as the administrative, business and judicial centers for the city—the place where legal matters were discussed and decided upon. The town gate was really another term for the town hall of ancient Israel. In Ruth 4:1, Boaz went to the town gate, knowing this was the place where witnesses were readily available. Boaz then called ten of the town elders to come to the gateway in order to make his case concerning Ruth. Therefore, at these gates or gateways, decision-making was undertaken, and elders and nobles would often convene there. The gates were guarded and protected because they gave entry into the political infrastructure of the city. It is not known if these gatekeepers had individual authority other than that delegated to them, but it appears that nobles, elders and high officials gave instructions to the gatekeepers— rather than receiving instructions from them.

From these and other scriptural references, we learn that gateways are places of entry and exit through which influence can come and go, and that gatekeepers had the responsibility for determining who entered and exited. If we accept that the physical realm is representative of the spiritual realm, then we can assume that even today there are spiritual gateways or portals throughout the world that inevitably influence nations and cities. Therefore, it is important to understand the function and authority of modern-day gatekeepers. In studying this concept in terms of revival, we must look at both the physical and spiritual realms.

Iniquitous Patterns Within Cities

Genesis 4 tells of the first two children belonging to Adam and Eve: Cain and Abel. Out of offense and jealousy, Cain chose to step outside the presence of God and murder Abel. Verse 8 says that Cain took Abel out to the field—the land—and committed the murder of his brother there. Already two major sins have occurred: bloodshed and covenant-breaking. In Genesis 4:17 we read that Cain became involved in building the first city. However, he was not doing this with God's authority, which means he was developing a precedent of city-building based on sinful behavior. A founder's behavioral pattern—whether it is one of poor stewardship or godly stewardship—can influence a city at every level of life. This earliest city was founded by Cain, who was in disobedience to God and murdered his brother. Cain's stewardship—or lack thereof—had the power to influence every component of city life and industry, which according to Genesis 4:20–22 included agriculture, industry, music and family development. Genesis 4:23 reveals that Lamech continued the pattern of murder and bloodshed, thus continuing the iniquitous pattern of sin handed down through successive generations from Cain.

Verse 25 says that Adam and Eve gave birth to Seth, who became the seed God used to deal with this iniquitous pattern. Shortly thereafter, people began to cry out and to call upon the name of the Lord (see verse 26). In other words, men were calling out for God to come to their city and visit them! This is perhaps one of the earliest examples of revival following the removal of Adam and Eve from the Garden of Eden. Man still had a desire to commune with God and wanted Him to be at the center of his life.

As we see in this first book of the Bible, cities are created for purposes. Gatekeepers need to be aware of the reason for which their cities were birthed in the first place. Was the city intended to be a place of commerce, music, entertainment, communication, agriculture or import and export? Understanding a city's purpose helps to define what sinful patterns accompanied its development over the years. Thus, the sinful behavior can be addressed by today's stewards of authority so that these earliest foundations will not continue to influence the city's ongoing life and development. To aid in this process, God places insight and vision within today's spiritual gatekeepers, or church leadership, to recognize such sin patterns. As Matthew 7:16-20 implies, corrupt roots—or foundations—always will yield corrupt fruit. Once the sinful roots and their subsequent corruption of society's foundations are pinpointed, the gatekeepers can deal with them accordingly. Once these gatekeepers begin to call out to God, the doors begin to open for God's purifying and redemptive presence to enter.

Global Gates

As cities developed over the years following the establishment of this first city, the role of the "gatekeeper" also developed. In a physical sense, these were the people who operated in high levels of industry, commerce, politics, finance, import and export, education, health and welfare—the "gateways" that still influence and affect people on a worldwide basis today.

As the world has continued to evolve in these areas, society has developed very specific global gates. Putting it simply, these global gates are seats of power from which people exercise authority both within their jurisdictions and beyond their jurisdictions in ways that affect the rest of the world. This concept is similar to the biblical descriptions of the city elders sitting at the gate and deciding who passes in and out, how taxes are handled, and which areas of law should be applied to legal situations.

In modern day terms the highest ranking of these gates would be the United Nations, the International Monetary Fund, the World Trade Organization, and what is referred to as the G8, a group composed of the seven strongest industrial nations—Britain, the U.S., France, Canada, Germany, Japan and Italy—and Russia. These "gates" hold all the power in finance and economy, among other things, on a worldwide basis. The weaker nations of the world tend to give away much of their sovereignty and power to these central global gates. In some cases, vast amounts of manipulation and compromise take place in high, but secretive, levels of decision-making. Often, the result is that some of the smaller nations have no choice but to give away their voice of disapproval or concern in return for whatever relief they receive—such as medical, famine or economic development assistance. The stronger nations can then impose educational or social demands upon the weaker nations, and often these demands are in direct opposition to Scripture. This is very challenging to a nation such as Uganda or Nigeria whose leadership seeks a return to godly values. For those of us who work in international prayer initiatives, this is one of our greatest concerns.

The Role of the Church in Gatekeeping

In the world today, the Lord has drawn the Church into a significant time of change. It is possible to change the entire spiritual climate of a nation through local and national prayer.

The *Transformations* videos are but one testimony of people of God around the world who are rising up and asserting their authority in the name of Christ to remove from their land whatever brings dishonor to the Lord. As we are now witnessing, entire nations, such as Uganda, are entering into covenants with God Himself. When considering the spiritual impact of such actions, it is easy to understand why so many changes are taking place in these nations at all levels of government, industry and church. This type of national change can take place only when the high-ranking spiritual leadership over a nation asserts that authority, such as the leadership of Uganda has done.

In this day and age, the Church is quite clearly rising up in nations all over the world in a way that missiologists have never observed before. This movement may well be the foreshadowing of what Jesus Himself promises in Revelation 5:7–14 and 7:9–10, that people from every nation, tribe and tongue will come to a living knowledge of the Lord.

Coming to such a knowledge means positioning ourselves at the global gates of the world and speaking forth His authority over all issues that affect His people in cities and nations worldwide. It means following through on the principles covered in this book and arriving at the place where we understand the level of authority that can be executed into the world through the leadership of the Church. It means standing in the gap for our communities, cities and nations, and petitioning the Lord for every person who wields any form of authority in government, law, education, industry, health, welfare, entertainment, etc. It means identifying any past iniquitous patterns that have been sown into the heart of our communities, cities and nations. It means praying with a new courage, believing that God will release His Kingdom authority into the lives of these people. God expects no less from His Church. With the cooperation of His Church, the Lord Himself can exercise spiritual authority over all the other kingdoms and nations in the world.

This is the high degree of commitment that God looks for from His people to ensure that His land will no longer be left in a position of desolation. "No longer will they call you Deserted, or name your land Desolate . . . for the LORD will take delight in you, and your land will be married" (Isaiah 62:4). This Scripture gives the impression of the land at every level—city, regional and national—being protected and cared for so that its destiny and purpose is fulfilled.

A Need for Spiritual Authority?

In revivals such as the Welsh Revival, covered in chapters 1 and 2, members of government, magistrates and judges, and those influential in business and economics were so involved in the revival itself that they would not even turn up at work. Why, therefore, did this revival come to an end?

The probable answer is that while the excitement and manifestation of revival was taking place, the Welsh church had difficulty sustaining the necessary prayer on a daily basis. Stewarding revival takes a great deal of work, especially when establishing revival at all levels of city and national life! In the case of the Welsh Revival, and in every case of revival in the history of mankind, there is a need for the Church to execute sustained spiritual authority. As the Church develops international ministerial and prayer fellowships, along with apostolic and prophetic councils of reference, and learns how to pray effectively at the global gates of the world, we will be executing just such spiritual authority on a worldwide basis. It is perplexing that we have not done so, but this is one of the main reasons national revivals have not been ignited, sustained and extended. Perhaps diagnosing why churches have not executed such authority might help to determine the solution.

One problem in executing spiritual authority is the nature of church leadership trying to work together. Although this is an essential element for revival and transformation, a number of challenges enter the picture. Often, for example, the most creative leaders simply do not participate, sometimes because of a higher call on their time from their own denominational jurisdictions. Some of these leaders will participate on an occasional basis, but then they are rarely involved in anything that is developing with maturity and vision.

Another problem is that ministerial fellowships tend to have more of an egalitarian mindset and become concerned if one person exercises strong leadership. Leaders often work independently and have a difficult time deferring to leaders of other denominations when they are used to calling the shots in their own particular denominational fellowship.

Another problem, as we have alluded to earlier, is that unity can become an end in itself without anything functional or directional ever emerging. Expressing relational unity requires some risk taking, such as undertaking prophetic acts throughout the city. Ruth Ruibal describes how the leadership of Cali, Colombia, undertook such an act when they released holy oil from a helicopter over the city!

An additional problem is that many ministerial fellowships work on the basis of courtesy rather than conviction. This is frustrating to pastors who are task-oriented, pastors who have mega-churches or pastors who need a little bit more expression in the course of decision-making!

Finally, many denominations require their pastors to leave their charge after a certain number of years. In such situations, those pastors may not exert spiritual authority because of a lack of territorial commitment, believing that they will be moving on to other fields in due course.

Authority comes from commitment to one's community, and the Church must develop more of an apostolic mentality in our communities, cities and nations. Only in this way can the Church establish authentic spiritual authority that is prepared to do what it takes to control the gates of our cities, our nations and the world—and thus, to experience the change that God waits for so patiently.

The Apostolic Paradigm

Developing an apostolic mentality enables the Church to see how revival can be stewarded into authentic transformation and can then permeate every part of society. But what does it mean to develop an apostolic mentality?

In recent years God has spoken clearly to His Church concerning the restoration of the gifts and in particular the office of apostle—in spite of some misgivings in several parts of the Body. It is not so much a question of restoring the office; rather, it is a matter of reactivating the function. Recognizing and utilizing the office of the apostle is vital to sustaining authentic revival.

Thus, the Church must understand what the role of the apostle involves. If an iniquitous pattern has influenced a community, city or nation for several generations, then a specific level of spiritual authority is required to disengage that pattern and to release the destiny and purpose of the Lord into that area. This requires the involvement of the apostle. The leaders of the church and the city can provide excellent research, tactics and strategy, but until the apostle is on board, they all will be pointing the weapons from their spiritual arsenals in different directions. In addition, while all pastors are leaders in their own constituencies, not every pastor is a city church leader. Pastors need focus and purpose if they are going to enter into any degree of relational unity, and this may well involve both personal and denominational repentance before a new foundation of trust and love can take place. The apostle brings that focus and purpose to the leadership of the Church. If the watchmen read the times and seasons in which we live and the prophets speak forth that word, then the apostle is the one to put it in order and settle it in the spiritual realm!

The office of the apostle, then, carries spiritual authority that is conferred by God Himself and supported by the Body of Christ. It is not based on performance or tenure or age but rather the ability to utilize maturity and wisdom and the willingness to understand the spiritual realm. Apostles need to be in a place of humility in order to affirm and encourage the rest of the leadership. When revival comes to an area, the apostle will understand the significance of stewarding the revival and sustaining it in order that God's purpose is fulfilled on earth as it is in heaven. Apostles in the church, in the marketplace, in politics and education, in health and in media, to name but a few stations, are all essential components of setting in order what God has established in heaven. Such apostles are "gatekeepers" and require the prayers and protection of the Body of Christ.

In places such as Argentina where revival has now been taking place on an ongoing basis for approximately twenty years, the apostolic order is in place. C. Peter Wagner addresses this revival in *The Rising Revival*:

> The shift from the traditional Christendom paradigm to the new apostolic paradigm, prominent in Argentina, is bringing with it the most radical changes in the way of "doing church," since the Protestant Reformation. . . . The

ongoing, mature, apostolic covering of the Argentine revival distinguishes it from many of the more short-lived revivals. One of the closest parallels might be the Wesleyan revival beginning in the 1730s in which John Wesley, Charles Wesley and George Whitfield were recognized apostolic figures who gave direction and government to the movement, which was sustained for decades.[1]

Pablo Deiros refers to the fact that the apostolic paradigm encompassed the first three centuries of Christian activity but has since been lost. Deiros points out that in the early years of the Church, Christians lived in a fairly hostile environment but understood the urgency of giving testimony and proclamation in the name of Jesus Christ and ministered with such authority that the signs of the Kingdom validated their proclamation. However, following the Edict of Milan in A.D. 313, when Constantine accepted Christianity as an official religion, the young Christian Church was no longer a persecuted minority. Deiros then says, "In this way the Church, the world and the Roman Empire turned out to be one and the same . . . it was no longer necessary for Christians to go to the world, because they were now part of it."[2] At this point, the identity of the Church changed, as well as its understanding of its mission, and mission itself was "abdicated to the hands of the established religious leaders."[3]

Ever since then the Church has been far more inward-looking than outward-looking. Until recent years, individual congregations and ministries focused primarily on the development and maintenance of their own programs and in-house strategies. They have been, therefore, less inclined to look at the bigger picture of what was happening in the world and unable to use that grid as a reference for decision-making. More recently, however, God has been challenging the worldview of the Church, stretching the Body to see its role far beyond that of its culturally accepted traditional parish or congregational boundaries. Consequently, the role of the apostle has taken on renewed significance for the Church in its call to spiritual gatekeeping—both locally and globally.

The Church today, therefore, is once again being challenged in new ways. The identity of the Church of Jesus Christ is changing, as we address these city, national and international gateways. The inward focus of dogmas and practices, denominational identities and in-house issues is beginning to give way once again to this apostolic paradigm. The Church is being repositioned back to its original call to address the world and its needs, and for that reason alone must shift into an apostolic mindset. This is what has been happening in Argentina and no doubt will continue to happen in other nations—such as Uganda— where apostolic leadership has begun to emerge.

A Foundation of Apostles and Prophets

If we follow through with some of the principles we have already addressed—such as the need for persevering leadership and prevailing prayer, and ensuring that there are no recurring footholds of sin—then we are in fact preparing the foundation for an apostolic ministry to develop that will give stability to the prophetic voice of the Church. These two roles work together to establish the Church in new wineskins that can adapt to the tasks of the Holy Spirit—intercessory prayer, spiritual warfare, spiritual mapping, and the healing of the land, for example. In these ways, spiritual strongholds over communities and cities—obstacles and impediments that bring offense to the Lord—are identified and removed. This is what prepares a city or a nation for revival. This is what enables the Church to pray with insight into iniquitous patterns and to remove them from the life and destiny of that city.

In Ephesians 2:20, Paul explains that the household of God has been built upon a foundation of apostles and prophets with Jesus Christ Himself as the chief cornerstone. Similarly, 1 Corinthians 12:28 states that God appointed first apostles then, second, prophets in a church. These roles need to be understood as foundational gifts for the Church today, and this is the order that is required for effective evangelism of the world.

Spiritual gatekeeping requires that the apostle and the prophet be recognized as integral components in addressing the affairs of the city and the world, and in releasing godly order. As a result, gatekeepers at all levels of society will more likely execute their areas of responsibility and decision-making under godly counsel and direction. Then the power and authority that God releases through gatekeepers who act on His behalf under His authority become the key to releasing His destiny upon the land. The Church must understand how to recognize and utilize these two offices in order to steward revival effectively and to ensure that the power of God's Kingdom is established.

12

...

Establishing Revival in Society

Whatever you bind on earth will be bound in heaven, and whatever you loose on earth will be loosed in heaven.

Jesus

Once revival takes place, it must be established. Unless we learn the principle of establishing or releasing revival into the core of society, it will not be sustained. This principle requires that all of the nine preceding principles studied in this book be in place. It also requires new, ongoing vision, willingness for a new wineskin and investment in the youth of society.

Second Chronicles 16:9 gives a timely reminder of the grace and favor that God is pouring upon the Church at this time: "For the eyes of the LORD range throughout the earth to strengthen those whose hearts are fully committed to him." The last few words of that verse also can be translated as: "to show Himself strong on behalf of those whose hearts are *loyal* to Him." If we can learn one thing from history, it is that God requires people who will embrace and nurture the seeds of revival that lead to lasting fruitfulness: faith, humility, repentance and prayer. Already we have seen that these are common denominators and foundations for each of the various principles we have examined.

One of the most costly mistakes made in all revivals is that many people became distracted by the effects of revival and, in so doing, lost sight of God's primary purposes for revival. This was the same concern Evan Roberts had during the Welsh Revival of 1906. Frank Bartleman, another man who was actively involved in that famous revival, had a similar perspective and sensed the imminence of God's visitation upon His people. He was concerned that many people missed this revival because they searched for it with their own agendas. He recognized that God required His Church to go into a time of travail and desperation and embrace a spirit of humility and repentance. It was essential for this depth of travail, humility and repentance to continue both prior to and during the revival, if the presence of God was to remain. He recognized that God was preparing the Church by releasing holy discontentment with its own impotence and spiritual barrenness. If revival was to come, the Church had to pray for a hunger regarded as radical. It still does.

Positioned for Entry

In Joshua 1:1–9 we read how God prepared Joshua to enter the Promised Land. It had been forty years since the initial attempted possession of the Promised Land. Joshua and his people knew their history, but they were ready for their destiny. He would personally lead his people into a new beginning and into the possession of their inheritance.

Joshua had waited for this moment for almost forty years. Before this entrance could happen, however, a spirit of unbelief had to be put to death following the negative report of the ten spies who saw only the giants of the land and ceased to recognize the sovereignty of God who was calling them into their destiny. Only Joshua and Caleb saw destiny beyond these "giants." In addition, before he could lead the people into the Promised Land, Joshua needed fresh passion and a fresh word from the Lord so that his "old wineskin" would not burst from the new responsibility and the increased faith, revelation and authority God was now giving him. For leaders in the twenty-first century Church, studying the history of Joshua—how he got to the point of entry into the Promised Land—is important because it illustrates two key principles that are necessary for transformation at any personal or corporate level.

First of all, we have to grow in what we sow. Exodus 33:11 says, "The LORD would speak to Moses face to face, as a man speaks with his friend. Then Moses would return to the camp, but his young aide Joshua son of Nun did not leave the tent." Joshua had watched and learned from his mentor Moses. He had learned that the secret of leadership is found in servanthood. He had been mentored by those who knew what it was like to meet with the Lord face to face. Joshua grew in what he had sown in servanthood and now he was applying it into his leadership.

Secondly, we grow to the degree that we sow in prayer. Joshua's desire was to die in the Promised Land, not in the wilderness, so he sought the Lord in prayer and had to wait until unbelief was put to death. Only after sowing in prayer could he finally take the people across the Jordan and into the land. He was not governed by the history of his people, but by the destiny He knew God had planned and promised for them.

In the same way, leaders today must sow in prayer. They must be persevering and bathed in prevailing prayer, surrounded by watchmen ministering in the spirit and power of unity, allowing no compromise of sin to interrupt their direction, willing to steward on God's terms whatever He gives them to protect, walking in the fear of the Lord, and learning how to occupy the gates of cities and nations. In other words, leadership today must grow through the sowing of prayer and must be governed by destiny—not simply by history. The crossing of any new Jordan requires that we understand our history and how it brought us to where we are. But seeking our destiny gives us vision and focus that is fueled by the Word of God. Walking in destiny involves heeding the Word of the Lord in one's heart and being obedient to Him—even if we have never gone in that direction before. When we sow in prayer, the Word of God becomes a lamp to our feet and a light for our path (see Psalm 119:105).

In addition to these two principles, the first nine verses in Joshua 1 give four more principles that offer a sense of direction in establishing revival in society today. First of all, we need to have *divine purpose* in our lives. Moses experienced such divine purpose, and while Joshua had witnessed this in the life of Moses, he needed it himself. Divine purpose had to be sown into his personal wineskin of leadership. Joshua had to be certain of the direction in which God was taking him, because leadership cannot afford to be anemic in its relationship with God. Being Scottish, I enjoy a good cup of tea, but invariably I visit places where the tea bag has had nothing more than a passing flirtation with the cup of hot water! The tea must be allowed to steep in hot water in order for the destiny of that tea bag to be fulfilled! And please do not give me a used tea bag. It has already lost its primary flavor! Joshua knew the purpose of the Lord because he knew and experienced the intimacy and intensity of His presence. It was fresh, it was urgent, and it was powerful. It was for his generation!

Secondly, Moses had been interested in *divine presence.* The apostolic leader must be a person of humility, holiness and true servanthood who is focused on the presence of the Lord. Learning from Moses' example, Joshua knew that in order for the full purposes of God to be manifested in the lives of His people, the presence of the Lord had to become a priority for each person. Only in this way could the people of God enter into their destiny—both individually and corporately. Each person in each tribe had to enter into the fullness of his or her destiny in order for the purposes of God in the lives of His people to be fulfilled. The prayer of the leader must be: "Lord, increase my appetite for Your presence in order that I understand Your purpose."

Thirdly, Joshua had to be ready for *divine position.* He had seen God's provision and faithfulness in the life of Moses, but he needed to hear the Lord's voice firsthand saying, "As I was with Moses, so I will be with you; I will never leave you nor forsake you" (Joshua1:5). The Promised Land was not entered into by "hearsay"; it was entered into by people who had heard God and responded accordingly. We may hear the word of the Lord through other people, as far as receiving direction for our lives is concerned. But we really need to hear and respond to it individually in order for it to permeate every part of our being. In this way, God positions us for action!

One final principle is that out of divine position comes *divine preparation,* and this principle is best gleaned from the account of David and Goliath. It was God who prepared David to meet Goliath, and David underwent at least three challenges in order for his apostolic wineskin to be put in place. He had to deal with the challenge of his family asserting that he was too young, then the challenge of the king that he had no experience, and finally the challenge of old equipment—Saul's armor—that did not fit the wineskin God had prepared for him. Once David overcame these challenges, God gave him the divine gift of grace, symbolized by the five smooth pebbles. Thus equipped, the appearance of Goliath did not intimidate David into thinking Goliath was too big to hit; rather, it reminded him that the giant was too big to miss since the Lord had prepared him for a time such as this. As God positions us for entry into the Promised Land, we will face challenges, and it is important for us to remember that God has divinely prepared us as well.

Although we discussed the concept of unity in chapter 8, I want to mention it here as well because lack of unity is such a major impediment to our entering the "land" God promised us. In reality, no new movement in history has developed out of unity, but rather out of *division*. Though we are called to walk in the spirit of unity, often only a small remnant will actually heed the word of the Lord for a new season. We need relational and Spirit-led unity—the type that perceives with the mind of Christ—but almost always there is an initial clash with an existing wineskin/mindset before the new direction unfolds. Paul says in 1 Corinthians 11:19 that divisions are necessary at times in order to determine any new direction God may be taking us, especially when it challenges what is familiar because what is familiar may not reflect God's glory for this next step. If we are operating with the type of unity that exists between the Father and the Son, then we also must separate ourselves from mindsets of disbelief that are trying to interrupt what God is calling us to undertake as He positions us for entry into the Promised Land.

Preparing the Next Generation

Rys Bevan Jones has stated: "Never let a generation grow up without that knowledge of Divine things which may contain the germ of national revival in years to come."

Authentic revival always includes young people at the forefront. History challenges us on this issue: "One distinctive feature of the Ulster Revival was the spiritual movement among children and teenagers. It was not uncommon for teenage boys to conduct street meetings among their peers. . . . At one such meeting, an Irish clergyman counted forty children and eighty parents listening to the preaching of twelve-year-old boys."[1]

On one occasion when Duncan Campbell was preaching a sermon, he paused and looked at one of the young lads in the congregation and sensed that the young man was in close contact with the Lord. He asked this young man, whose name was Donald McPhail, if he would be willing to lead the congregation in prayer:

The young man rose to his feet . . . he began to sob, and lifting his eyes toward heaven, cried, "Oh God, there is power, let it loose!" The spirit of God swept into the building and the heavens were opened. The church resembled a battlefield. On one side many were prostrated over the seats weeping and sighing; on the other side some were affected by throwing their arms up in the air in a rigid posture for an hour. God had come.[2]

The power of youth at prayer—amazing! Exciting! Profound!

When revival comes into a community, the pulsating power of God will affect everything in that place. This is the time to prepare the next generation. Proverbs 22:6 says, "Train a child in the way he should go, and when he is old he will not turn from it." This particular verse of Scripture is not limited to an individual. It is a spiritual truth that is equally applicable to cities and nations. When any body, city or nation is trained in the ways of the Lord, then understanding, expectation and the authority of the Lord are released. The principle encapsulated in this verse is required for the stewarding of God's presence. *It is the one that is most overlooked, but it is also the one that can have the most impact upon an entire nation.* Simply put, this principle is the establishment of revival in society through the modeling and teaching of our young people.

Part of the instruction God gave Joshua as he was about to enter the Promised Land was: "Be careful to obey all the law my servant Moses gave you; do not turn from it to the right or to the left, that you may be successful wherever you go. Do not let this Book of the Law depart from your mouth; meditate on it day and night, so that you may be careful to do everything written in it. Then you will be prosperous and successful" (Joshua 1:7–8). It has always been God's intention for the next generation of leadership to be taught the ways of the Lord. This was part of the instruction given for proper stewardship. Moses said:

These are the commands, decrees and laws the LORD your God directed me to teach you to observe in the land that you are crossing the Jordan to possess, so that you, your children and their children after them may fear the LORD your God as long as you live by keeping all his decrees and commands that I give you, and so that you may enjoy long life. Hear, O Israel, and be careful to obey so that it may go well with you and that you may increase greatly in a land flowing with milk and honey, just as the LORD, the God of your fathers, promised you.

Deuteronomy 6:1–3

It is quite clear that the Lord wants each generation to be well birthed and "earthed" in His relationship with all of society. Duncan Campbell puts it this way:

After all, the greatest contribution you or I can make to the cause of Christ is the impact of our unconscious influence, and that influence impregnated by the life of Jesus. We will have failed in our object, unless we bring back to our schools, our colleges, our homes and our common task, something of the uncommon fragrance of Jesus.[3]

Discipleship through Christian education is a powerful way of stewarding revival right in the heart of a nation. This means changing the "three Rs" to the "four Rs": reading, writing, 'rithmetic and revival! History records the impact that revival can have upon an education system. The Korean Revival, for example, profoundly influenced the Christian colleges of the nation. Records indicate that "ninety percent of the students at Union Christian College in Pyongyang professed conversion in February 1907. Many also sensed God's call upon their lives as evangelists. They carried the revival beyond the city and into village churches throughout Korea."[4]

However, it was the ultimate impact upon the entire population of Korea that was so significant. Towns and Porter point out that those young missionaries required illiterate Korean adult converts to read Korean, albeit in a simplified version, before being admitted to membership in the Christian Church. Furthermore, Christians had to be distinguished from Japanese collaborators, and so had to recite chapters from the Bible to prove their Christian faith. "The result was a 100 percent literacy rate among Christians in a largely illiterate nation. Their ability to read made Christians the natural leaders of the Korean society."[5] Those students discipled in the knowledge of the Lord ultimately influenced the leadership of the nation itself!

A number of similar examples in the more recent history of revival testify to the fact that educating people in the knowledge of the Lord affects society at all levels. In Great Britain, the Welsh Revival influenced the morality of a generation as reflected in a reduction in crime and an increase in honesty and chastity throughout the nation. In America, revival produced "a revival of righteousness that culminated with the passing of the Eighteenth Amendment to the United States Constitution. Furthermore, pupils attending Christian schools in India . . . doubled in the two decades following the revival. . . . In China, missionaries laid the foundations of that nation's educational and medical systems. The same was true in many nations throughout the African continent.[6]

In another recent example, Harold Caballeros, pastor of El Shaddai Church in Guatemala City, Guatemala, was seeking the Lord's wisdom about taking the Gospel to his entire nation. The Lord spoke clearly: "I will reveal to you the most powerful weapon in the possession of a nation—Christian Education."[7] God continued to speak to Caballeros on this subject. Says Caballeros, "God's next two arguments were impressive. The first was clarifying the mistake of the Christian Church, which consists of 'going for yesterday's generation and not for the future one.'"[8] Shortly after this revelation, Caballeros visited Wales and was concerned to find that many of the beautiful Welsh church buildings that blossomed during the time of the Welsh Revival were now being used for other purposes such as restaurants; and some had even become mosques. How could this have happened when such a vast number of people had been converted during the revival? In essence, no stewardship for the future had taken place during the Welsh Revival. Caballeros goes on to say, "If we do not invest in affecting the next generation, if we do not educate children in God's Word, then every time a generational cycle starts we have to evangelize again the children of those who were believers. This makes it very difficult to 'make disciples in all nations.'"[9]

In recent days, Harold Caballeros has shared some exciting, revolutionary steps he has begun to undertake with senior advisors in the fields of psychology and education to introduce Christian education into every level of life in Guatemala. In the last 25 years or so the Christian population of Guatemala has risen from 2 percent to approximately 47 percent. Some believe that with Christian influence in the educational system that statistic will rise in the next few years to 60 percent or higher.

Is it possible to take the Gospel of Christ into the core of learning in our nations? As Caballeros points out, if we are unable to do this, then revival will be condemned to exist for only one generation—and then the whole procedure must start all over again. If we are truly going to have an impact for Christ on our communities, then it is important that our prayer teams are vigilant and consistent in praying for schools, colleges and the overall education system. Caballeros says, "Christian education is a way of assuring that the revival will affect future generations. The reformation and restoration of a community are ways of measuring the impact of revival."[10]

Is it possible to Christianize an entire nation? The Japanese Business and Economic System always plans twenty years in advance. Advance planning means they factor everything that happens *today* into a meaningful foundation and investment that will bear much fruit later. The Christian mandate is to do no less, and even now to be preparing for revival in such a way that it will influence civilization even a hundred years from now—or until Jesus returns.

We have learned that authentic revival leads to restoration, when the people of God go back to a place of intimacy with the Lord in order to experience fruitfulness in their lives—the type of fruitfulness that remains. When we start taking the impact of revival into the heart of the educational system, it in essence changes the way people think, so that as these people mature and enter different facets of society, society as a whole becomes impregnated with the Gospel of Christ and begins to think with the mind of Christ. In this way, mindsets that hold cities and nations in bondage can be removed and replaced with the higher purposes of the living God.

Damazio says that today "we have a generation that desperately needs an encounter with an authentic Christ, an authentic church and authentic spiritual mentors and leaders."[11] He continues with a quote from George Barna who expresses sentiments representative of today's Generation X: "Searching desperately for godly mentors to teach us, yet not knowing where to look, we are feeling like runners stranded at the starting gate without a baton . . . ours is a traumatized generation, lacking direction and identity—missing a sense of continuity with our heritage."[12]

I serve as part of a leadership team with Watchmen For The Nation. This ministry seeks to have the glory of the Lord restored among His people in order that His resting place can be found in our midst. Over the years this ministry has engaged in many acts of reconciliation and restitution in what are termed as Gatherings, venues during which thousands of people simply wait upon the Lord as He directs the course of events. In Canada this has included times of ministry between the French and the English, between the native and non-native, and between the Jewish people and Canada as a nation, which dealt with the issue of Canada sending many Jewish people back into the Holocaust at a time when they needed Canada's protection and hospitality.

While all of these examples are powerful and still being walked out and stewarded, perhaps the most significant occasion took place recently at a venue in Atlantic Canada involving more than two thousand people. We had a time of reconciliation between the older generation and Generation X, in which the younger generation was released into its call of leadership upon the land. Significant repentance, forgiveness and reconciliation took place between both groups. In the end the power of God's presence was quite extraordinary as these young men and women people took their place and, in turn, began ministering to and releasing the generation that followed them, as well as blessing the older generation. Each generation honoring and releasing the generations that follow is a key principle toward establishing God's presence and power upon the land and throughout society.

None of us in this generation, young or old, can afford to miss the revival rivers as they begin to flow in our direction. As Frank Damazio says in *Crossing Rivers, Taking Cities*:

> When a generation reacts to or misses the river of God, it may be a Judges 2:10 generation; "Another generation arose after them who did not know the Lord, nor the work which He had done for Israel." Reverend Bevon Jones states, "Never let a generation grow up without that knowledge of divine things which may contain the germ of national revival in years to come!"[13]

The Fruit of Established Revival

Real revival is one that results in lasting transformation in every facet of society. This is why we pray for those in authority over us. This is why we pray for members of the G8 nations and for the United Nations. This is why we pray for those who are regarded as apostles in the marketplace, apostles in the field of education, apostles in business and commerce. We pray for all of these authority figures because when *they* are under the authority of Christ and have the mind of Christ, then the Lord is able to execute His purposes in a way that reflects His presence and His glory throughout society.

When the 1948 revival began in the Hebrides, it swept across the land touching homes, businesses, schools:

Fishermen out in their boats; men behind their looms; men at the pit bank; a merchant out in his truck; schoolteachers examining their papers were gripped by the power of God, and by ten o'clock the roads were streaming with people from every direction, making their way to the church . . . the town was changed, lives and homes transformed, and even the fishing fleet as it sailed out into the bay took with it a Precenter, to lead them in prayer and worship singing.[14]

True revival affects everything in society!

Once today's Church understands that it has entered into the same covenant that was given to Abraham when he was called to be a blessing to all nations (see Genesis 12:2–3), a covenant that was reaffirmed by Jesus and commissioned to His Church, then our purpose is clarified in being called to bless the nations in the name of the living God. Only an authentic spiritual revival will make this possible. Only the stewarding of such a revival will result in the removal of sinful foundations, the (re)establishment of godly values and lasting fruit that reflects the beauty and majesty of God as Lord of the nations.

Nothing is impossible with God! Psalm 33:12 says it beautifully: "Blessed is the nation whose God is the LORD, the people he chose for his inheritance."

13

...

Releasing Our Destiny

This is what revival is all about—a personal visit from the One who loves us, who died for us, who was raised for us, who intercedes for us, and who now lives within us. Every personal encounter with our wonderful Savior brings the invitation, "Follow Me, and I will make you fishers of men."

Bill Bright

God has a destiny for His people—as individuals and as entire nations—even as war rages over the people of God. It seems improbable that a revival releasing the presence of God among His people can actually be interrupted or stopped by the enemy of our souls. Yet, history has proven that revivals come and revivals go, and often they leave because the people of God are not obedient to or do not fully cooperate with the Holy Spirit, or they are not fully aware of the consequences of spiritual opposition. Paul the apostle says something of significance in this respect, since all sorts of incidents—people, authorities, spiritual conflict—prohibited him from doing the work He believed God had called him to do: "For we wanted to come to you—certainly I, Paul, did, again and again—but Satan stopped us" (1 Thessalonians 2:18).

Spiritual conflict is real, and it is this type of conflict that will interrupt any outpouring of the living God upon our lives. We need His presence to go with us if we are going to experience His rest. Remember the conversation between Moses and God: "The Lord replied, 'My Presence will go with you, and I will give you rest.' Then Moses said to him, 'If your Presence does not go with us, do not send us up from here. How will anyone know that you are pleased with me and with your people unless you go with us?'" (Exodus 33:14–16). As did Moses, we too realize that we must have His presence with us, but we also must know how to steward that presence. In doing so, not only can we ensure the visitation of His presence, but we also can ensure the continued habitation of the Lord with His people.

We can learn from the experience of history, and in so doing, we have defined ten means by which we can engage in this spiritual conflict and win. These ten principles we have addressed give us guidelines and parameters for maintaining, sustaining, retaining and extending the glory of His presence.

Expectancy, Availability and Repentance

One day the granddaughter of Duncan Campbell came to his study and asked him, "Why doesn't God do the things today that you talk about in your sermons?"[1] Campbell was immediately convicted and fell on his face before the Lord crying, "Lord, if You will do it again, I will go anywhere to have revival."[2] It is really all a matter of availability and expectancy. Not long after, God called him to the church in the Hebrides. Of course, several people in the Hebrides already had been praying for revival, waiting on the Lord and expecting Him to move in great power. Thus, as the Lord moved some to pray, He also caused a young girl to go to her grandfather with a question that challenged Campbell's life and ultimately motivated him to do the work God called him to do.

So expectancy and availability are vital to welcoming God's presence, but one other ingredient is also common to every known historical revival. At the start of the 1936 New Zealand Revival, J. Edwin Orr spoke at a convention in Ngaruawahia. He challenged the people present, asking if they really felt God was going to give them revival. When they said "Amen," Orr responded, "But do you believe that He will start a revival here in this tent tonight?" After a moment of silence, one young man answered quietly, "*If we pay the price.*"[3] Revival started the moment people began to confess their sins.

As you have been reading this book I trust that, like myself, you have heard the challenge from the Lord once again: Do we want Him to send revival? Have we invited His presence into our cities and our nations? G. Campbell Morgan once said, "Revival cannot be organized, but we can set our sails to catch the wind from heaven when God chooses to blow upon His people once again."[4] When we choose to repent and seek His face, when we enter into a season of meaningful prayer, and when we are available and expectant, the presence of God is ready to meet with us.

From the very beginning of Scripture we find that God longs to meet with us. He wants to release hope in us and to take us back to our point of departure from Him, thus transforming the lives of His people. God wants to reinstate us into the depth of intimacy with Him that Adam and Eve experienced in the Garden. We know that this revival is possible, because Jesus was born, died and was resurrected—and so opened the way for us to experience intimacy with the Lord. Revival starts with our saying *yes*. When we focus on Him and make Him our passionate desire, God will trust His presence in our midst. Then He can pour His expectancy into our lives and revival can actually begin!

Frank Damazio quotes the English writer, the late Arthur Wallis:

> Revival is divine intervention in the normal course of spiritual things. It is God revealing Himself to man in awesome holiness and irresistible power. It is such a manifest working of God that human personalities are overshadowed and human programs are abandoned. It is man retiring to the background because God has taken the field. It is the Lord working in extraordinary power on saint and sinner. Revival accomplishes what our best spiritual efforts cannot.[5]

Revival proponents from the past, such as Wallis, and present-day proponents, such as Damazio, are saying the same thing—that revival is a sovereign work of God that brings refreshing to the Church. It often results in significant repentance and humility and may cause the Church to look at new wineskins of discovery. Since it is a time of refreshment and rediscovery of lost intimacy, it is also a time of preparing us for destiny.

Praying Destiny—Not Despair

In chapter 4 we looked at Hannah as a person who prayed for the destiny of her life to be fulfilled. Even in her time of barrenness she was full of expectancy. Her prayers were not birthed out of despair, but out of expectant hope that God would fulfill her destiny. She faced the impossible and the improbable, but her travail and her tenacity released her destiny because she said *yes*. Even Eli, who represented the Church in the day of Hannah, misunderstood her posture and attitude (see 1 Samuel 1:13–15). However, Hannah would not accept the conditions at hand as her destiny; she believed that God would fill her barren womb. Similarly, today is a season of new wineskins in the Church, and we must be full of expectancy that the presence of the Lord will fill our barrenness.

Another element in the life of Hannah is important for us to heed as the Church in the twenty-first century. Once she received her destiny, Hannah then shared it with the rest of the land. Even as Hannah gave away Samuel, the beginning of 1 Samuel 2 notes that she was overwhelmed with joy. As a result, Samuel became part of God's wider plan for the people of that day. In the same way, when individuals, cities and nations receive the inheritance of our destinies, we must be willing to share it with others. After the conception comes the sacrifice. God knows the disposition of our hearts and whether or not we are willing to give away what we are called to birth. This is a critical part of revival, since out of revival comes harvest and growth. We must be willing to give away, or share, our destiny.

There also needs to be a desperate desire for that destiny. Hannah was *desperate* for her destiny, and it was this desperation that led to her expectancy. As is shown in the life of Hannah, when we pray with desperation God is able to position us to see His city and His nation through His eyes. Once we are given this revelation, then we embrace it wholeheartedly and pray with unceasing expectation.

The Womb of Expectancy

Hannah's desperation led to conception. It was the same with other women in the Bible who were in a place of barrenness. Into them, God planted His seed of hope and destiny and impregnated it with the power of the Holy Spirit.

Abraham laughed at the thought of his barren Sarah giving birth (see Genesis 17:17). But upon this covenantal promise, Isaac was indeed born, and God's promise of destiny was fulfilled. And just as Hannah gave away Samuel, her destiny, for the Lord's purposes, Abraham and Sarah were also tested in their willingness to hand back Isaac to the Lord.

Similarly, Manoah's wife was barren (see Judges 13), and even when she told him that the angel of the Lord had visited her, he did not believe. He requested a second visit from the angel. Even though Manoah perceived in the natural, his wife was able to perceive in the spiritual. She, too, gave birth—to Samson.

A third example is Elizabeth, the wife of Zechariah, who gave birth to John the Baptist in her old age. They had to commit him into the hands of the Lord, as well—in the same way that Manoah and his wife gave Samson—so that the purposes of God could be fulfilled through their son.

Each of these women represents the Church and God's plan to take the Church into the next wineskin of birth, ministry and destiny. We must be sure that we do not despise or disbelieve what God wants to release in our midst. Disbelief, improbability and impossibility must be addressed on occasion, but in the end, the empty, barren womb gives birth in accordance with God's promise.

The Bible also gives an example of a woman who tried to block the reviving power of God's presence from entering the city and as a consequence became an offense to the Lord. King David's wife Michal despised her husband for the manner in which she celebrated the presence of the Lord entering the city (see 2 Samuel 6:16, 20–23). Because of her offense, "Michal the daughter of Saul had no child to the day of her death" (verse 23). We must watch that no offense remains within us or upon the land that could impede His reviving presence coming into our midst.

Michal's reaction to her husband's passion for the Lord's presence is perplexing. Commenting on an observation once made by Floyd McClung, that Michal's reaction was possibly that of a woman involved in a dysfunctional marriage and that she could have been jealous based on the little time David spent with her and ministered to her needs, Steve Fry makes an interesting point.[6] As Fry says, any "jealousy, envy and competition actually reveals a lack of love for God. If we love Him, we will long for His presence, and if we long for His presence, we will want His dwelling place to be established—with us fitting where He wants us to fit."[7] How important it is to have no such pattern of insensitivity or lack of communication in the preparations we undertake to welcome the Lord's presence!

Today, God is clearly birthing something profound in the spiritual realm.

How pregnant are you with vision and expectancy? Can you see the manner in which God wants to birth something new in your life, your church fellowship, your city and your nation? Is there offense in your life that may prevent God from birthing revival in you? Preparation is involved, and we have work to do. May we allow Him to plant a seed of anticipation, perseverance and purity into the womb of *our* faith, so that we may behold the release of His destiny for us and the falling of His glory upon us.

The Power of Forgiveness

Before God can plant such seeds in our lives, however, we may need to receive the power of His forgiveness so that we can walk with holiness and humility in His presence. People who walk in the presence of the Lord must also be willing to walk in the power of forgiveness.

Several Scriptures speak profoundly to the subject of the power of forgiveness. In Genesis 33 we read of the wonderful reconciliation between Esau and Jacob, when Esau runs to forgive Jacob for having stolen his birthright. In that reunion Jacob bows seven times to the ground in search of forgiveness, and in so doing melts Esau's heart and is promptly reconciled with his brother. Such is the power of forgiveness. Genesis 45 tells of a similar reconciliation between Joseph and his brothers. Joseph asks his brothers not to be angry with themselves for their betrayal of him since God obviously had a higher plan and destiny through all that had taken place (see Genesis 45:1–7). The power of forgiveness, then, releases the *peace* of God.

Jesus once said something that at first appears confusing: "Do not suppose that I have come to bring peace to the earth. I did not come to bring peace, but a sword" (Matthew 10:34). Yet, in John 14:27, Jesus says, "Peace I leave with you; my peace I give you. I do not give to you as the world gives." Jesus is not contradicting Himself. He is, in fact, establishing a standard that is essential for us to understand if we want His sovereignty and His presence to be at work in our lives. It is a standard that models the perspective of the Kingdom of God for all our relationships and priorities, as opposed to the thinking of the world, thereby releasing the hallmark of the Lord.

In Matthew 18, we see the authority God assigns to His Church:

> "If your brother sins against you, go and show him his fault, just between the two of you. If he listens to you, you have won your brother over. But if he will not listen, take one or two others along, so that every matter may be established by the testimony of two or three witnesses. If he refuses to listen to them, tell it to the church; and if he

refuses to listen even to the church, treat him as you would a pagan or a tax collector. I tell you the truth, whatever you bind on earth will be bound in heaven, and whatever you loose on earth will be loosed in heaven. Again, I tell you that if two of you on earth agree about anything you ask for, it will be done for you by my Father in heaven. For where two or three come together in my name, there am I with them." Then Peter came to Jesus and asked, "Lord, how many times shall I forgive my brother . . . ? Up to seven times?" Jesus answered, "I tell you, not seven times, but seventy-seven times."

Matthew 18:15–22

In verses 18 and 19, Jesus gives extraordinary promises that when we agree about anything we ask for it will be done for us, and that when we come together in His name, God will be in our midst. But notice what follows. After this promise, Peter asks Jesus about the issue of forgiveness, and Jesus responds that the depth and quality of forgiveness we must have for each other is limitless. This is the power of forgiveness that then releases the *presence* of the Lord. Those promises of Jesus rest upon our willingness to give and receive forgiveness.

"Have faith in God. . . . I tell you the truth, if anyone says to this mountain, 'Go, throw yourself into the sea,' and does not doubt in his heart but believes that what he says will happen, it will be done for him. Therefore I tell you, whatever you ask for in prayer, believe that you have received it, and it will be yours."

Mark 11:22–24

But note that this marvelous promise ends with a reminder: "And when you stand praying, if you hold anything against anyone, forgive him, so that your Father in heaven may forgive you your sins" (Mark 11:25). This passage could better be translated from the original text to indicate that if we have the faith of God at work in us, we can face any obstacle or adversity and dismiss it in the name of Jesus—so long as we are operating in the power of forgiveness. The power of forgiveness literally releases the *power* of the Holy Spirit in our midst.

In John 20:21–23 the resurrected Christ is talking to His disciples. He speaks peace into their lives and sends the disciples (and us) into the world with the same terms of reference that His Father sent Him. He breathes on them and tells them to receive the Holy Spirit. Then He adds, "If you forgive anyone his sins, they are forgiven; if you do not forgive them, they are not forgiven" (verse 23). This practice of being sent out in the name of Christ, with the peace of Christ and with the authority of Christ is, therefore, based on the power of forgiveness. The power of forgiveness, then, also releases the *practice* of Christ into our lives.

Second Corinthians 2:10–11 says, "If you forgive anyone, I also forgive him. And what I have forgiven—if there was anything to forgive—I have forgiven in the sight of Christ for your sake, in order that Satan might not outwit us. For we are not unaware of his schemes." When we walk and live in the position of forgiveness and are willing to receive forgiveness ourselves, then not even the enemy of God's people can outwit us, since God alerts us to his schemes. This is the *perspective* of Christ for living in the Kingdom of God.

Scripture is clear, therefore, that forgiveness releases the peace of Christ, the presence of Christ, the power of Christ, the practice of Christ and the perspective of Christ. In addition, over the centuries revival has occurred when people began to recognize that forgiveness and reconciliation are initial and essential steps in preparation for His presence. The power of forgiveness, then, is absolutely necessary to the release of revival and the continued stewardship of God's presence in our lives.

Rise and Walk

We are being positioned today for what will probably be the most extraordinary time in Church history. Many believe that we are living in the generation that may witness the return of the Lord Jesus Christ. Yet Scripture is clear that we are to keep doing the work of the Kingdom of God until He returns, in spite of whatever challenges we may encounter. God is waiting for His Church to rise up and walk into the destiny He has planned for us.

Luke 6 describes the man in the synagogue whose right hand was shriveled. Even though the Pharisees and the teachers were looking for further evidence to trap Jesus and find Him guilty of breaking their laws, Jesus simply looked at the man and told him to "get up" (verse 8). In this passage, the man with the withered hand serves as another metaphor of the Church. Jesus is commissioning the twenty-first century Church to get up, to be willing to confront whatever giants are facing us and to do what is necessary to welcome the presence of the Lord into our midst.

In the biblical sense, standing up means to be willing to intercede and stand in the gap (see Ezekiel 22:30). But Jesus also asked the man to do it in front of everyone! It is as if Jesus is exposing and highlighting our vulnerability. He wants to remind us that in our weakness His strength is made perfect. This was a destiny moment for this man—and it is a destiny moment for the Church. When Jesus told the man to stretch out his right hand, he was asking him to expose his point of weakness, his frailty, his inability, the area he never wanted to have exposed.

Today, Jesus is exposing a myriad of issues in His Church because He longs for us to have His strength pulsating through every part of our being. "My power is made perfect in weakness" (2 Corinthians 12:9). And as the man stretched out his area of vulnerability, Jesus restored the strength to his hand. Jesus discomforted his comfort zone, inconvenienced the man's status quo and challenged his life of mediocrity. But in so doing, Jesus was able to pour His life-giving, restoring Spirit into the man's life. It is the same for us in the Church today. Jesus is waiting for us to rise up and stand, to stretch out our hands and to be willing to relinquish our vulnerability in order for His sovereignty to be released. No more mediocrity!

Acts 3:1–10 gives another powerful picture of the Church in the twenty-first century rising to enter into its destiny. Peter and John meet a man at the Gate Beautiful. The man has been crippled from birth and is used to a life of professional begging. Peter and John tell the man that they have neither silver nor gold, but they do have the name of Jesus Christ. They help him up by the right hand—the symbol of power and authority—and they tell him to walk. What a lesson for us today! It is time for the Church to rise up and walk, to stop begging and to start appropriating the riches and resources of the Kingdom of God, and then to start releasing them into a needy world. Like the crippled beggar, let us now be prepared to walk into our destiny and seek the reviving power of the Lord for this century.

A Time for Realignment

Occasionally my car requires a wheel realignment and re-balancing to keep it from heading toward the shoulder of the road. Similarly, biblical revival gives and requires necessary correction or re-direction to ensure that the Church continues in the direction established and empowered by the Lord.

I appreciate these words of Frank Damazio: "Revival redesigns us with the power and presence that could and should be the norm for a Church functioning in the Spirit with the same power of the Early Church. The Church today should walk in that level of New Testament Christianity, whether in revival or out of revival."[8] Damazio makes an interesting point when he says, "Revival must be absorbed into truth. Without this we will be forced into fabricating a revival atmosphere.[9]

For this reason, revival needs to be founded upon the Word of God and not upon experiential motivation. When revival is based purely on something emotional or experiential, its season will not last long. In spite of its influence throughout the world, one of the criticisms against the Welsh Revival—and in particular Evan Roberts—was its tendency toward the emotional. Obviously there will be a degree of emotion when the Holy Spirit works in our lives, but we need to learn how to walk in the power of the Holy Spirit with and without emotion. This develops maturity and integrity. It also enables the Church to sustain its influence and the presence of Christ in society in a way that is well-grounded and balanced.

Damazio also states, "Revival spirit cooperates with biblical truth, which sustains the life flow of the Holy Spirit. A healthy church that has established the unmistakable permanent truths clearly laid out for us in Scripture will receive more from a revival season than a non-prepared Church.[10] Revival, therefore, is a time of "repositioning" for the Church that enables us to retain a contemporary and prophetic voice for whatever challenges we face in society. This means that we will continue to rely upon the ongoing work and life of the Holy Spirit, who has promised to guide and direct us into all truth.

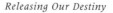

Again, to quote Damazio: "There is nothing that will drive the next generation away from God more than dead, learned spiritual behavior. A new season does not mean we must lose what has been gained during revival. It simply means we must sustain what has been gained by new application."[11] It is for this reason that I believe the influence of revival can be sustained from one generation to another. If we follow and apply the principles outlined in this book and dutifully establish them in our personal lives, the lives of our local church fellowships, the life of the city church and the life of the nation, then we can live in a society that is under the influence of the council of the Living God and that seeks His counsel at all levels of life.

The result will be similar to the sentiment of the Christian worker in Uganda to whom I referred in chapter 1 who, when asked to describe the revival and transformation currently taking place in his nation, replied that he was not aware of any particular degree of transformation taking place that was different from normal life. His experience of daily life included people being saved, healed and delivered, with an ongoing change of ethics and morality in all spheres.

My belief is that revival *can* be sustained with the presence of God continually being poured out upon society. It is also my firm belief that God is now realigning and positioning His Church for the next revival and is challenging us to learn the principles of stewarding His revival in advance so that the full effect of the revival fulfills His purposes in the world at this time. If we read the signs of the times correctly, then we can recognize that the next season of revival soon will be upon us, and it will be our responsibility to steward it wisely, carefully and prayerfully, since God has entrusted this high measure of responsibility to His Church.

The Signs of the Times

As mentioned in my earlier discussion of Luke 6, the authorities of Jesus' day regularly tried to accuse Him of breaking some regulation or law. Their testing of Jesus in this manner also is described in Matthew 16, where Jesus makes an interesting comment about the end times: "You know how to interpret the appearance of the sky, but you cannot interpret the signs of the times" (Matthew 16:3). Jesus continues, "A wicked and adulterous generation looks for a miraculous sign, but none will be given it except the sign of Jonah" (verse 4). We all know the story of Jonah and how God used him as His servant to prepare Nineveh for an awakening. While the awakening did not last, it was nevertheless an indication of God's love and vision for that city.

Matthew 24 gives further information about the end times. For me, the critical passage is verse 14: "And this gospel of the kingdom will be preached in the whole world as a testimony to all nations, and then the end will come." Of course, many other passages in the Bible can be viewed in an apocalyptic sense to explain the end times and when the return of Christ might take place. But my personal belief is that Matthew 24:14 is the litmus test for understanding the times in which we live. During recent years, as I have traveled, researched revival and participated in the work of God's transforming power in cities and nations, I have sensed a growing expectation of coming revival that will result in a great harvest. This harvest may well usher in the return of Christ. Present-day indicators point toward a revival of national and international proportion, the likes of which we have not yet seen, but that appears to be on the horizon.

The number of prayer movements on a worldwide basis has increased significantly over the last several years. In Canada alone more than twenty national prayer movements have individual mandates but work together from time to time. This development is similar in many other nations. On a worldwide basis we are witnessing an increasing awareness of city reaching and city transformation—a challenge for those trained in older wineskins who are being stretched to go beyond their local church fellowship and to recognize the reality of pastoring a city. The city church is composed of many participating congregations all contributing their wonderful emphases and uniqueness. The liturgical church joins hands with the charismatic church, which joins hands with the Pentecostal church, which joins hands with Word of Life church and the Full Gospel church and so on. The Church at large is increasingly recognizing the need to be in fellowship.

There is also an increase in martyrdom for Christ, as well as an increase in the willingness to be martyred for Christ. Over the years, an increase in the spirit of martyrdom has been indicative of a renewed courage within the Church and a daring willingness to face adversity and challenge with inspired vision. Along with this trend is an increase in worldwide intercession. Literally millions of intercessors are now praying on a daily basis for the fulfillment of the Great Commission, and many are linked to prayer centers through computers, e-mail and other forms of modern technology. This phenomenon has never happened before to such an extent.

Spiritual mapping—otherwise known as cultural geography, cultural anthropology or spiritual epidemiology—has become a discipline of prayer that is now used in many facets of the Christian Church all over the world. Now taught as an elective subject in some schools of mission, Bible Colleges and even seminaries, this practice of informative prayer is a new wineskin for many but is teaching the Church how to pray on-site with spiritual insight that would otherwise have been difficult to diagnose. In addition, the number of unreached people groups is dwindling; we could soon see the Gospel in the hands of those that remain and watch as church fellowships are established in their midst. Many people sincerely believe that the Great Commission is now within reach and that the prophecy of Matthew 24:14 may be fulfilled in our lifetime.

But other issues also enable us to read the signs of the times. For example, as September 11, 2001, portrayed so vividly and as we see almost every day in the news, the world has entered the era of international terrorism. The Church must respond to this threat accordingly. Another issue is the heightened battle against humanism and relativism, which the Church is fighting even within her own ranks. Just today I read a report in which one of the largest denominational churches voted on whether or not their clergy can bless same-sex marriages, and the motion was passed with a strong majority. The pressure of the world is on the Church to sink into the ocean of relativity. It is essential that the Church not conform to the world (see Romans 12:2), but that the world see the Church as the living Body of Christ, promising a hope and a future (see Jeremiah 29:11). The words of Isaiah 5:20 are alarmingly accurate for the world today: "Woe to those who call evil good and good evil, who put darkness for light and light for darkness, who put bitter for sweet and sweet for bitter."

Charles Finney was asked the question concerning when to expect a revival. To summarize his response, he said that when the Church truly grieves over the wickedness of sin and willingly enters into a time of repentance, and humbles itself before the Lord on this issue, and truly prays for revival, then the Lord is positioning His Church for a divine encounter.[12] Finney also said when people are willing to do whatever God wants in order for His reviving presence to come, then revival is near. Whenever I travel these days, I find that the word *revival* is almost always on people's lips and that a hunger for revival is rapidly accelerating. These are the signs of the times.

Are You Ready for the Challenge?

If we truly want to have the abiding fruit (see John 15:4) that Jesus wants us to experience and share, then we need to abide in His presence. This intimacy with the Lord—both in experience and expression—must go beyond head knowledge to heart knowledge. If we truly are willing to pay the price and do whatever is necessary for revival to enter our midst, then God is "able to do immeasurably more than all we ask or imagine" (Ephesians 3:20). However, we must prepare, be disciplined and be willing to pay the price. In this day and age, when the Church is engaging in the final frontier of mission, a much more aggressive battle is taking place in the spiritual realm. Before we act, we need to have ears and eyes that can interpret the times in which we live and listen to what the Lord is saying.

The persevering Church is the Church that will open the door to the presence of the Lord and welcome Him into our communities. We must be ready to persevere in what God is about to release into our care. And we must recognize that whatever door He opens, no man can close—but also, whatever door He closes, no man can open. In trying to negotiate the spiritual contours of challenge that face us, we need to seek the wisdom of God Himself and not the wisdom of man, a program or even the Church. We must not attempt to do this in our own human strength and wisdom, for there is too much at stake. Delays and disappointments need to be interpreted as seasons that are required for transformation and redeployment in the way we go about the business of the

Church today. While this is challenging, it is essential if we are to understand the urgency of the hour in which we live.

Harold Caballeros believes that the story behind the ongoing transformation of Almolonga, Guatemala, is the fact that they followed the pattern of discipleship and prayer as found in Acts 19. This was then "followed by a consistent practice of deliverance ministry . . . this open heaven brought a great freedom for evangelism . . . the resulting revival transformed the life and the culture . . . even . . . so far as to affect the natural elements, making Almolonga the most fertile land in the whole country."[13]

In summary, the ten simple principles that comprise the body of this book can be found in communities such as Almolonga, or nations such as Uganda, or any place that God's people are willing the make the sacrifices necessary to welcome the presence of the living God—including wherever you or I live.

1. Be a persevering leader and do not give up, even when the enemy throws the worst he can at you. Be steadfast, apply the full armor of God, surround yourself with seasoned and mature intercessors and remember that nothing is too hard for the Lord (see Genesis 18:14). He can birth a new seed even in the most barren of wombs.

2. Be a person of prevailing prayer. Allow the Lord to take you into a discovery of prayer where you meet with Him in that most holy place. Expect to experience the giants that oppose revival, since usually they will remain disguised or hidden until serious prayer exposes them in the light of Christ. Resist the temptation to end the momentum of prevailing prayer. In the process of such prayer, you will be challenged at the place of greatest vulnerability, and it is at this point that revivals can either be ignited or defused.

3. Understand what it is to live in the fear of the Lord and experience the intimacy that brings pleasure both to God and His people. In this place of intimacy, we will experience impunity in the Lord and His promise that "no weapon forged against you will prevail, and you will refute every tongue that accuses you. This is the heritage of the servants of the LORD" (Isaiah 54:17). When we live, work and worship in the fear of the Lord, we receive His wisdom: "Fear of man will prove to be a snare, but whoever trusts in the LORD is kept safe" (Proverbs 29:25).

4. Resist sin at all levels and at all costs. If we want to sustain the holy presence of the Lord in our midst, there is no room for compromise. We must be vigilant and allow no footholds of compromise to engage or ensnare us.

5. Choose to become stewards of the territory assigned to our care and custodianship. We are called to restore those boundaries and foundations that God has entrusted to us to guard, keep and occupy.

6. Understand the power of unity that authenticates the voice of the Church in society today. Even as our eyes are fixed on the Lord Jesus (see Hebrews 12:2), divisions and differences inevitably will occur (see 1 Corinthians 11:18–19). Unity is vital to prepare us for the new wineskin required for the task at hand.

7. Engage in acts of kindness that so motivated and empowered Jesus Himself, releasing His compassion and the power of the Kingdom of God into the hearts and lives of a needy society. God will reveal to us what those acts of kindness may include, depending upon the unique needs that exist in our individual communities, cities and nations.

8. Enlist the ongoing and ever-increasing role of watchmen, since increased territory means increased responsibility. We cannot all be watchmen, but some are called

specifically for this purpose—and these people are found in every church, community, city and nation. Ask the Lord for these people to be released, and He will show them to us. It is then our responsibility to train and equip them so that they continue to stand in the gap on behalf of the leadership and the Lord Himself!

9. Seek to restore the apostolic leadership that is so necessary for this day and age—and, in particular, the office of the apostle. The apostle is one who must walk in humility, holiness and integrity without selfish ambition, and who is raised up and affirmed through the rest of the leadership. But the apostle is also well aware of the need for an "every member ministry." Several revivals over the last two centuries never really allowed for proper equipping within the Body of Christ. Revival will not be sustained when we look to an individual rather than to the whole measure of ministry of God through His Body. As Frank Damazio puts it, we need to remove "the myth of the 'man of God' syndrome."[14] Duncan Campbell was well aware of this point and made it clear that he did not bring revival. Therefore, watchmen discern the times, the prophet speaks it forth and the apostle sets it in order with the full agreement of the Body of Christ. Without this divine order in place, disorder will soon result.

10. Finally, it is our responsibility—and a critical spiritual principle—to establish revival in society. This means experiencing a fresh ongoing vision of the Lord in our lives every day. It means allowing the new wineskins to develop. It means investing in the lives of our children and teenagers. Our children and grandchildren are the David and Joshua generations of today who are more than able to enter the front

lines, but they require our mentoring, our protection and our time. As a leader, whom are you mentoring at this moment?

Are you passionate for revival in your own life? Are we passionate for revival in the lives of our local church fellowships? Are we desperate enough to pray for revival in the communities and cities in which we live and work? Are we courageous enough to pray for revival to arrest the heart of our nations?

And the real question is, are we ready for the challenge?

The Fire Must Not Go Out

The twenty-first century Church faces many challenges. On September 11, 2001, a change in the "spiritual plates" of this world occurred. The age of innocence was over, the wake-up call was made, and the Church was placed in the gap and told to speak the Word of God into the heart of the world. A fresh encounter with the Living God is now at hand.

In Old Testament days, the burnt offering was a serious part of encountering and maintaining intimacy with the Living God. The requirement God gave to His people was this: "The fire on the altar must be kept burning; it must not go out . . . The fire must be kept burning on the altar continuously; it must not go out" (Leviticus 6:12–13). This perpetual fire on the holy altar represented the ongoing and uninterrupted offering made to God on behalf of the people. Offerings were made every morning and evening, and double offerings were offered on the Sabbath. Furthermore, anybody could make a special burnt offering to express his devotion to the Lord. The Hebrew name for this offering means "going up," which symbolizes the power of worship and prayer ascending to the Lord from His people. The altar was set near the entrance to the tabernacle. It was an offering based on thanksgiving and praise and was an acceptable sacrifice to the Lord that brought Him honor and glory.

Paul urges us to offer ourselves as living sacrifices, people who are holy and pleasing to Him (see Romans 12:1). Such sacrifice brings immense pleasure to God, and as a result He promises to meet all our needs according to His glorious riches in Christ Jesus (see Philippians 4:18–19). Jesus Himself modeled the power of making an acceptable sacrifice to God, and we are called to be imitators of this practice (see Ephesians 5:1).

To steward revival, to steward the presence of God, to steward the glory of God is a high calling requiring the full sacrifice of our hearts and lives. Nothing less will do. The Lord is waiting to release His presence and to let His glory fall. Our prayer can simply be one of invitation, expectancy and anticipation: "Lord, come and make us Your dwelling place." For this reason, *the fire must be kept burning on the altar continuously; it must not go out.*

He has called us to keep the fire burning.

Notes

Chapter 1

1. David Pawson, "Follow Where the Spirit Leads," *Renewal Magazine*, April/May 1986, Anglican Renewal Ministries, Haddenham, Bucks, U.K., 12.

2. Frank Damazio, *Crossing Rivers, Taking Cities* (Minneapolis: Regal Books, 1999), 79.

3. Ibid., 79–84.

4. Ibid., 81.

5. John Ferguson, ed., *When God Came Down: An Account of the North Uist Revival, 1957-58* (Drumsmittal, Scotland: Lewis Recordings, 2000), 15–16.

6. Gerald Fry, *In Pursuit of His Glory* (Tacoma, Wash.: Mount Hermon Press, 1999), 45.

7. V. Raymond Edman, *Finney on Revival* (Minneapolis: Bethany, 2000), 80, 107.

8. Colin Dye, *Revival Phenomena* (Tonbridge, U.K.: Sovereign World, 1996), 12.

9. Ibid., 10.

10. Fry, *In Pursuit of His Glory,* 45.

11. Ibid., 45.

12. Richard F. Lovelace, *Dynamics of Spiritual Life* (Downers Grove, Ill.: InterVarsity Press, 1979), 52.

13. A definition adapted from a taped message delivered by Duncan Campbell to students of the Faith Mission Bible College in Edin-

burgh, Scotland. Full details of the ministry of Duncan Campbell can be found in the archives of this college.

14. Duncan Campbell, *The Price and Power of Revival* (Edinburgh, Scotland: The Faith Mission), 29.

15. Ibid., 56.

16. Kathie Walters, *Bright and Shining Revival* (Macon, Ga.: Good News Fellowship Ministries, 2000), 8–10.

17. Ibid., 21.

18. Desmond Cartwright, *The Real Smith Wigglesworth* (Kent, England: Sovereign World, 2000), 23.

19. Walters, *Bright and Shining Revival,* 1.

20. Elmer Towns and Douglas Porter, *The Ten Greatest Revivals Ever* (Ann Arbor, Mich.: Servant Publications, 2000),

21. Walters, *Bright and Shining Revival,* 1–2.

22. Rev. Owen Murphy, *When God Stepped Down from Heaven,* (Macon, Ga.: Good News Fellowship Ministries, 2000), 3, quoted in Walters, *Bright and Shining Revival,* 3.

23. Towns and Porter, *The Ten Greatest Revivals Ever,* 34.

24. Ibid., 44.

25. Based on my personal conversations with Ruth Ruibal.

26. Statistics received in conversation with Harold Caballeros, senior pastor of El Shaddai Church in Guatemala City.

27. Alistair Petrie, *Releasing Heaven on Earth* (Grand Rapids: Chosen Books, 2000), 178–207.

28. J. Lee Grady, "Nigeria's Miracles," *Charisma & Christian Life,* May 2002, 44.

Chapter 2

1. George Otis, Jr., *Informed Intercession* (Ventura, Calif.: Renew Books, 1999), 60.

2. Roy Fish, quoted in John Avant, Malcolm McDow and Alvin Reid, eds., *Revival!* (Nashville: Broadman and Holman, 1996), 152.

3. Ibid.

4. Fry, *In Pursuit of His Glory,* 15.

5. Ibid., 29–32.

6. Petrie, *Releasing Heaven on Earth,* 219.

7. Fry, *In Pursuit of His Glory,* 33.

8. Ibid., 33.

9. Frank Damazio, *Seasons of Revival* (Portland: Bible Temple Publishers, 1996), 409.

10. Fry, *In Pursuit of His Glory,* 34–43.

11. Edman, *Finney on Revival,* 132–38.

12. Leonard Ravenhill, *Why Revival Tarries* (Minneapolis: Bethany, 1959), 55–56.
13. Ibid., 57.
14. Ibid., 55.
15. Fish in Avant, McDow and Reid, *Revival!*, 153.

Chapter 3

1. Tom White, *City-Wide Prayer Movements: One Church, Many Congregations* (Ann Arbor, Mich.: Vine Books, 2001), 166.
2. Ibid., 167.
3. Petrie, *Releasing Heaven on Earth*, 53–82.
4. Fish in Avant, McDow and Reid, *Revival!*, 153.
5. Harold Caballeros and Mel Winger, eds., *The Transforming Power of Revival* (Buenos Aires: Editorial Penier, 1998), 15.
6. Steve Fry, *Rekindled Flame* (Sisters, Ore.: Multnomah, 2002), 177–83.
7. Ibid., 179.
8. Ibid., 180.
9. Ibid., 183.

Chapter 4

1. C. Peter Wagner and Pablo Deiros, *The Rising Revival* (Ventura, Calif.: Renew Books, 1998), 7.
2. Ibid., 10.
3. Ibid., 14.
4. Ibid., 15.
5. Walters, *Bright and Shining Revival*, 42–46.
6. Campbell, *The Price and Power of Revival*, 56.
7. Colin N. Peckham, *Heritage of Revival* (Edinburgh, Scotland: The Faith Mission, 1986), 165.
8. Ibid., 166.
9. Brynmor Pierce Jones, *An Instrument of Revival* (South Plainsfield, N.J.: Bridge Publishing, 1995), 36.
10. Ibid., 38.
11. Towns and Porter, *The Ten Greatest Revivals Ever*, 42.
12. Ibid., 42.
13. Ibid., 43.
14. Ibid.
15. Fry, *Rekindled Flame*, 193.
16. Otis, *Informed Intercession*, 83.
17. Ravenhill, *Why Revival Tarries*, 23–24, 83.

Chapter 5

1. *Concise Oxford Dictionary,* 5th ed. (London: Oxford University Press, 1911), 1964, 565.
2. Ibid., 709.
3. Fish in Avant, McDow and Reid, *Revival!,* 157.
4. Fry, *Rekindled Flame,* 31.
5. Ibid., 32.

Chapter 6

1. Justin Long, "Whatever Happened to Lamentation?" *Charisma,* May 2002, 71.
2. Fish in Avant, McDow and Reid, *Revival!,* 155.

Chapter 7

1. James Strong, *The New Strong's Exhaustive Concordance of the Bible* (Nashville: Thomas Nelson, 1990), 2421.
2. Charles G. Finney, *Lectures on Revival* (Minneapolis: Bethany, 1988), 15.
3. Wagner and Deiros, *The Rising Revival,* 44–45.
4. Martin Scott, *Sowing Seeds for Revival* (Tonbridge, U.K.: Sovereign World, 2001), 83–87.
5. Ibid., 84.
6. Ibid., 85.
7. Petrie, *Releasing Heaven on Earth,* 200–201.
8. Scott, *Sowing Seeds for Revival,* 85.
9. Ibid., 86–87.
10. Ibid., 87.
11. Strong, *The New Strong's Exhaustive Concordance,* 5432.
12. E. C. W. Boulton, *George Jeffreys: A Ministry of the Miraculous* (Tonbridge, U.K.: Sovereign World, 1999), 36.
13. Ibid., 33.

Chapter 8

1. *Every Day with Jesus,* May/June 2002 (Farnham, U.K.: Crusade for World Revival). Reading for June 7, 2002.
2. Ruth Ruibal, *Unity in the Spirit* (Lynnwood, Wash.: Transform-Nations Media, 2002), 56.
3. Ibid., 29.
4. Ibid., 31.
5. John D. Robb and James A. Hill, *The Peacemaking Power of Prayer* (Nashville: Broadman and Holman, 2000), 9.

6. Ruibal, *Unity in the Spirit,* 37.
7. Campbell McAlpine, *Explaining Loyalty, Betrayal and Offense* (Tonbridge, U.K.: Sovereign World, 1994), 23–24.
8. Ibid., 45–46.
9. Fish in Avant, McDow and Reid, *Revival!,* 156.

Chapter 9

1. C. Peter Wagner, *Revival! It Can Transform Your City* (Colorado Springs: Wagner Institute for Practical Ministry, 1999), 44.
2. Ruibal, *Unity in the Spirit,* 71.
3. Ibid., 60–61.

Chapter 11

1. Wagner and Deiros, *The Rising Revival,* 19.
2. Ibid., 47.
3. Ibid., 48.

Chapter 12

1. Towns and Porter, *The Ten Greatest Revivals Ever,* 125.
2. Walters, *Bright and Shining Revival,* 14.
3. Campbell, *The Price and Power of Revival,* 20.
4. Towns and Porter, *The Ten Greatest Revivals Ever,* 44.
5. Ibid., 45.
6. Ibid., 53–54.
7. Caballeros and Winger, 19.
8. Ibid., 9.
9. Ibid., 19.
10. Ibid., 20.
11. Damazio, *Crossing Rivers, Taking Cities,* 97.
12. Ibid., 97, quoting Barna Research Paper, taken from a pre-published manuscript
13. Damazio, *Crossing Rivers, Taking Cities,* 65.
14. Walters, *Bright and Shining Revival,* 15–16.

Chapter 13

1. Towns and Porter, *The Ten Greatest Revivals Ever,* 146.
2. Ibid., 146.
3. Ibid., 142.
4. Ibid., 201.
5. Damazio, *Seasons of Revival,* 10.
6. Fry, *Rekindled Flame,* 162.

7. Ibid., 185.
8. Damazio, *Seasons of Revival,* 401.
9. Ibid., 401.
10. Ibid., 404.
11. Ibid., 408.
12. Finney, *Lectures on Revival,* 23.
13. Caballeros and Winger, 21
14. Damazio, *Seasons of Revival,* 200–208.

Bibliography

Avant, John, Malcolm McDow and Alvin Reid, eds. *Revival!*. Nashville: Broadman & Holman, 1996.

Boulton, E.C.W. *George Jeffreys. A Ministry of the Miraculous.* Cambridge, Kent: Sovereign World, 1999.

Caballeros, Harold and Mel Winger, eds. *The Transforming Power of Revival.* Buenos Aires: Editorial Penier, 1998.

Campbell, Duncan. *The Price and Power of Revival.* Edinburgh: The Faith Mission, nd.

Cartwright, Desmond. *The Real Smith Wigglesworth.* Tonbridge, Kent: Sovereign World, 2000.

Charisma & Christian Life Magazine. May 2002.

Concise Oxford Dictionary. London: Oxford University Press, fifth ed., 1964.

Damazio, Frank. *Crossing Rivers, Taking Cities.* Regal Books, 1999.

————. *Seasons of Revival.* Portland: Bible Temple, 1996.

Dye, Colin. *Revival Phenomena.* Kent: Sovereign World, 1996.

Edman, V. Raymond. *Finney on Revival.* Minneapolis: Bethany House Publishers, 2000.

Every Day with Jesus. Farnham England: Crusade for World Revival, May/June 2002.

Ferguson, John, ed. *When God Came Down (An account of the North Uist Revival, 1957-58).* Drumsmittal, Lewis Recordings, 2000.

Finney, Charles G. *Lectures on Revival.* Minneapolis: Bethany House, 1988.

Fry, Gerald. *In Pursuit of His Glory.* Tacoma, 1999.

Fry, Steve. *Rekindled Flame.* Sisters: Multnomah, 2002.

Jones, Brynmor Pierce. *An Instrument of Revival.* South Plainsfield, NJ: Bridge Publishing, 1995.

Lovelace, Richard F. *Dynamics of Spiritual Life.* Inter-Varsity Press, 1979.

McAlpine, Campbell. *Explaining Loyalty, Betrayal & Offense.* Tonbridge, Kent: Sovereign World, 1994.

Otis, George Jr. *Informed Intercession.* Ventura, CA: Renew Books, a Division of Gospel Light, 1999.

Peckham, Colin N. *Heritage of Revival.* Edinburgh: The Faith Mission, 1986.

Petrie, Alistair. *Releasing Heaven on Earth.* Grand Rapids, MI: Chosen Books, 2000.

Pratney, Winkie. *Revival Principles and Principalities.* Lafayette: Hunting House, 1944.

Ravenhill, Leonard. *Why Revival Tarries.* Minneapolis: Bethany House,1959.

Renewal Magazine Edition # 122, April/May 1986, Haddenham, Bucks: Anglican Renewal Ministries, Tacoma, WA, 1999.

Robb, John D. and James A. Hill. *The Peacemaking Power of Prayer.* Nashville, TN: Broadman & Holman Publishers, 2000.

Ruibal, Ruth. *Unity in the Spirit.* Lynnwood, WA: TransformNations Media, Division of Sentinel Group, 2002.

Scott, Martin. *Sowing Seeds for Revival.* Tonbridge, Kent: Sovereign World, 2001.

Strong, James. *New Strong's Exhaustive Concordance of the Bible.* Nashville: Thomas Nelson, 1990.

Touch Point Bible, New Living Translation. Wheaton, IL: Tyndale House Publishers, 1996.

Towns, Elmer and Douglas Porter. *The Ten Greatest Revivals Ever.* Ann Arbor, MI: Servant Publications, 2000.

Wagner, C. Peter. *Revival! It Can Transform Your City.* Colorado Springs, CO: Wagner Institute for Practical Ministry, 1999.

Wagner, C.Peter and Pablo Deiros. *The Rising Revival.* Ventura, CA: Renew Books, a Division of Gospel Light. 1998.

Walters, Kathie. *Bright and Shining Revival.* Macon GA: Good News Fellowship Ministries, 2000.

White, Tom. *Citywide Prayer Movements-One Church, Many Congregations.* Ann Arbor, MI: Vine Books, Servant Publications, 2001.

Index

Rev. Dr. Alistair P. Petrie was born in Scotland and raised in Canada. He was ordained into the Anglican Church in 1976 in York, England. His doctor of ministry degree was undertaken through Fuller Theological Seminary in the area of spiritual issues in church growth. He has since ministered in parishes in both England and Scotland, as well as through his most recent position as rector of Brentwood Anglican Chapel, Brentwood Bay, British Columbia, for more than fifteen years. He is married to Marie and they have two sons, Michael and Richard.

Alistair left residential ministry in June of 1997 in order to become the director of Joshua Connection Canada, a mission ministry serving the broader Body of Christ. He later became the director of international operations for the Sentinel Group and the executive director for Sentinel Ministries Canada, and now is the executive director of Partnership Ministries, a Canada-based ministry serving the Church around the world. He currently serves on various ministry boards and is an associate faculty member for the Wagner Leadership Institute, as well as a guest lecturer at Fuller Theological Seminary. He is involved in various prayer initiatives currently taking place in several parts of the world.

Alistair has been a proponent of renewal and evangelism in the Anglican/Episcopal Church for many years and has been involved in conference and mission work as a plenary speaker and workshop leader throughout North America and overseas, having ministered across many nations on six continents.

Alistair's main thrust of ministry in recent years has been in helping the Church discover the cutting-edge insights of turning an entire community toward Christ in order that the community, the city, and the nation can be positioned and prepared for revival. He gives instruction in the biblical understanding of the stewardship of land and the effect this has on people, churches, communities and cities. Through this teaching it becomes possible to diagnose through historical, cultural, physical and spiritual research the bondages and wounds in an area that often impede effective evangelism. He has developed this teaching utilizing the tools of intercession, spiritual warfare, spiritual mapping and commitment to the land—essential components in liberating and transforming a community into Christ.